T0155399

The Scent of Lemons

The Scent of Lemons

*Technology and relationships
in the age of Facebook*

Jonah Lynch

DARTON·LONGMAN + TODD

First published in 2012 by
Darton, Longman and Todd Ltd
1 Spencer Court
140–142 Wandsworth High Street
London SW18 4JJ

Copyright © 2012 Jonah Lynch

The right of Jonah Lynch to be identified as the Author of this work has been asserted
in accordance with the Copyright, Designs and Patents Act 1998.

ISBN: 978-0-232-52958-6

A catalogue record for this book is available from the British Library.

Extract from 'The Dry Salvages' taken from Four Quartets
© Estate of T.S. Eliot and reprinted by permission of Faber and Faber Ltd.

Designed and typeset by Kerrypress Ltd, Luton, Beds.
Printed and bound by Bell & Bain, Glasgow

□ □ □

CONTENTS

PREFACE

Outside my window, there is a lemon tree. For more than ten years I have been living in this house in Rome, and yet still I feel a sense of wonder when I see the bright yellow of the lemons on the tree. For someone like me, who grew up in a colder climate, citrus trees have something miraculous about them. They fill the greyest, coldest days of the year with glowing colours and delicious flavours. They are like storage tanks for the sun, which they treasure up for the days when we need it the most.

I have always loved lemons. When I was a child, my aunt would offer me candies and I always chose the yellow ones. Sometimes they were banana flavoured – gross! – but usually they had that sweet-sour taste of lemon. When I got sick, my mum prepared mugs of hot lemon-and-honey. Now, when I walk in the garden, I often stop to smell the clean and lively scent of a just-picked lemon.

But what do lemons have to do with technology? A lemon fresh from the tree has a rough skin. The better the tree has been cared for, the rougher it is. It's a strange roughness, because if you squeeze the lemon a little, a perfumed oil comes out and makes the skin suddenly smooth to the touch. And then there's that wonderful sour juice, so good on fish and oysters, in summertime drinks and in a hot cup of tea! Touch, scent, taste. Three of the five senses cannot be transmitted through technology. Three-fifths of reality, sixty per cent.

This book is an invitation to notice the sixty per cent.

I

□ □ □

SETTING THE SCENE

1

BEGINNINGS

I wish someone else were writing this book. I find myself in front of a series of subjects on which I am no expert. Yet what follows is not an exercise in vanity. I feel the urgent need to clarify my relationship with the technologies which in ever more elegant and hidden ways accompany our lives. I feel this need so strongly that I publish these incomplete thoughts now, and would be willing to go back and correct them if necessary, if to do so would bring about a more profound dialogue on technology and human relationships.

I believe this dialogue should happen now. It should happen between the people of my generation and that which precedes mine; between the people who arrived early into the world of computers but who remember how the world was before: the people who today are the teachers, professors, parents, priests – the educators. In a decade or so it will be a bit late for serious reflection. Direct experience of the world before the internet will be lacking, and that will make it hard to have the serenity of a point of view not entirely predetermined, because not entirely immersed in the world it attempts to critique. Those born in the age of the internet cannot be their own teachers. It is up to us, their fathers and mothers and older siblings, to reflect on the meaning of the inventions that we have brought to be, and which are having a profound influence in every part of daily life.

I would like to arrive through successive approximations at a description of my starting point, using a readily understood dichotomy: the 'Luddites' and the 'Progressives'.

On the one hand we have the Luddites. Remember old Ned Ludd? With some of his friends, angered by new fabric production technologies in England at the beginning of the nineteenth century, he became the near mythical figurehead of a sometimes violent insurrection against automation in the cotton and wool mills of Britain before government intervention declared damage to property of this kind a capital offence. He represented a man of the people, and wanted to protect skilled workers who were about to lose their jobs and their craft because of the introduction of new wide frame automated looms into textile factories. In a certain sense, one can sympathize with his aims, but the ways he tried to achieve them were rather less acceptable. Besides the blind violence and damage done to innocent persons, his position was unacceptable because it did not offer any real alternative. Technologies generally arise from a positive desire: to work with less effort; to produce more with the same resources; to produce more, more quickly. They do not arise out of a diabolic desire to put down the common man. If they have this effect, the solution should not be sought in the destruction of what has come into existence.

On the other hand we have the 'Progressives'. These are the people who embrace every scientific discovery and think the power unleashed by technology will always be used for good. They do not want rules or limits. They think it will be the evolution of the species to guide the use of technology. Although they have undergone several setbacks during the twentieth century, they still remain a sizeable group. Let's briefly recall that towards the end of the 1800s it was commonly thought that we were about to arrive in the 'promised land', the end of every religion and lasting world peace, because of scientific discoveries.

And then the First and Second World Wars broke out, and then the Cold War with the terrible possibility of a nuclear conflict, and finally the incompetent cynicism that dominates the political discussion of today. This is at least enough to say that progress is certainly not always linear, nor is it is always positive.

From the refusal of progress another ideology arose, and in some parts of our society still prevails, one which we can superficially identity with many attempts to return to the earth, to a simpler life ('small is beautiful', the hippy movements, and so on). Technological progress, it is decreed, is carrying us farther from the beauty of nature and the immediacy of human relationships; we should therefore escape the world of technology to recreate paradise lost on a hill in the forest. But this, too, does not lead anywhere, and it also commits the sin of ingratitude for the many tools that technology has given us. It is all very well to live 'the simple life' when one has good health, but it is rare to find a hippy ready to die rather than go to the doctor. When homeopathic remedies do not work, western medicine is just fine.

The world which these movements oppose, however, does not lack for problems. It is clear that capitalism tends to produce huge waste and ugliness. Moreover, capitalism requires constant acceleration in order to generate and to satisfy an ever growing number of desires. In this regard we are living in an eloquent moment of realism. The economic crisis which broke out in 2008 is a rather strong condemnation of the idea that selfishness can become a virtue through the alchemy of finance.

To return to the actions of Ned Ludd and his kind, we can see how a troubling misunderstanding has arisen: that anyone who questions technology is deep down a Luddite or a nostalgic, a hippy in sheep's clothing. This misunderstanding is blinding us. It is impeding us from considering freely one of the most important questions of our time. The absence of balance generates ideology, and ideology impoverishes both those who win the argument and those who lose it. This book is a small contribution toward a more reasonable and constructive conversation.

Many others are writing about technology and reality, neuroscience, learning and human relationships. What do I have to add to the debate? Two things above all. In the first place my insistence on freedom and self-determination. Fate does not exist. I am allergic both to nostalgic discourses, as if the past was always better than the future, and to the enthusiastic and a-critical arguments which face the future with the blind positivity of a lemming. We are talking about *which* future we want to live, and to decide that, we need to consider all the available data.

Second, I give the opinion of a Christian. This is a voice often on the periphery with respect to a prevalently scientific and philosophic subject, but in the debate on technology it can offer an original contribution starting from the incarnation, the exaltation of the physical world. In the heart of the book I will try to follow this path, in particular with respect to human relationships. What is the difference between laughing in the company of friends, and writing 'hahahaha' on a chat screen? What does it mean for adolescent friendships, when Nielsen discovered in 2010 in the US that adolescent girls sent on average 4050 SMS a month, and the boys 'only' 2539 messages?[1] What type of communication can happen in 160 characters? What gets left out?

□ □ □

2

A NERD'S LIFE

My uncle gave me a PC when I was only 7. It was a wonderful TI 99/4A. Like many of the first PCs, you connected it to a television screen, and used a normal cassette tape player as a disk. In the same year, 1985, I learned to program in BASIC. Then in high school I learned C++ and Pascal, and at the university Fortran and Java.

I liked to play with graphics, and in particular with fractals, which I found fascinating for their link between mathematics and powerful calculating machines, and I delighted in the surprising beauty of the pictures produced. I was the first in my high school to have a modem. Already at the beginning of the 1990s, I was playing around on the local bulletin boards, where I would chat about the things that interested me with people I had never met. In 1994 I got my first email address. Like many nerds of the time I chose the name of an obscure Shakespearean character as my user name. Then it was time to look for software on FTP – file transfer protocol – and to chat with people ever further away on IRC – internet relay chat.

The web already existed, although I had never used it; only in 1996 when at university did I discover it. But using chat I met someone my age from Finland, with philosophical interests, who knew English quite well, and we spent a few months exchanging almost daily messages, on the existence of God, good and evil, and art. Every once in a while I am reminded of these exchanges;

alas I did not save any of them, and I do not remember the unpronounceable name of my virtual friend to look for him on Facebook.

During the last year of high school I took an online course, *Introduction to Philosophy,* offered by the local university through their bulletin board. Here too, I never actually met the professor, except on chat or email. As is clear by the theme of the course and of the lost messages, there was another thing that fascinated me during these years besides technology: the life of the spirit, the intellectual life. That interest first brought me to philosophy, then to the Catholic faith, and finally I entered a seminary.

During my college years and the first two years of seminary I lived without a computer. A laptop cost too much and in any case I did not really need one. Of course, I compulsively checked my email on the computers in the university lab.

But in 2002, beginning my third year in seminary, I felt a strong desire to have a computer again. I saw all of my friends with wonderful laptops capable of doing amazing things, so for Christmas I asked my parents to buy me a Toshiba. It was not the latest model, and it was heavy and too large, but somehow it was beautiful and it was mine.

Straightaway I got into the habit of downloading the PDF of the Vatican newspaper every evening. My Toshiba was an iPad before its time. Five pounds of steel and glass on which I could listen to Mozart while reading about the latest goings on in the Catholic world at seven in the morning, as I rode the bus to the university.

At university I took notes on my laptop. It was certainly easier to copy them, share them, and look for key words, if the texts were in electronic format. I am pretty quick at typing like many young Americans – from an early age I learned to touch-type –

still, it remained very difficult to keep up with a lecturing professor. Some of them spoke slowly, but most said too many things to transcribe everything. On my laptop I quickly realized lectures were all the more difficult to summarize and while I forced myself to continue with it for a few weeks, I soon left the laptop at home and returned to my handwritten notes.

In any case, I spent a lot of time with my new machine away from lectures. There were stacks of CDs to copy or to convert into mp3 files, immense prairies on the internet to wander through, programs to search for that promised to save me a lot of time. (Although, if I add up the time spent searching for them and testing them, I do not know if I actually saved any whatsoever.) Since it was a Windows machine, every three or four months I had to reformat the disk, reinstall everything, and start over.

The first time was fun, like cleaning out the garage when I was young. The second time not so much … Then there were viruses, spyware, updates, licences to crack. I found my life invaded with little battles to fight, and spent hours on maintenance to enable the proper functioning of the machine. I started to long for a better computer, one less open to attacks and instability. So I read all the internet forums I could find, and after six months of weighing up the possibilities, in the end I decided I would buy an iMac.

□ □ □

Oh, Macintosh, iMac of my heart, how I appreciated your simple elegance, your obsequious speed! New computer, new life! And since I was still a student, those nice guys at the Apple store gave me a free iPod with the purchase of my computer: I hurriedly stuffed it with bytes and bytes of music, and went out on my bike.

At first, it was wonderful. With a soft aria playing, riding my bike was like flying. Then the 'soundtrack effect' got me a little too excited and I made some swerves between buses and cars that almost cost me my life. I took off the iPod, trembling, and I have not put it on since while cycling!

I worked a lot with my iMac, writing tons of pages of reports every week for the university, as well as preparing lessons for the high school where I worked teaching physics. And then there was the television series *24* on Monday night! I could not miss it: after one episode in the company of Jack Bauer I was hooked. That was fine until a friend gave me all the previous seasons of *24* on DVD! One disk, three episodes, 120 minutes each disk, 8 disks per season. And I saw every one of them. I watched the episodes while studying, in a window on my computer. It was great to be able to jump over the boring parts, like the scenes with Jack's daughter, a girl who is always whining. But in jumping between the video, the book that I was reading, the text I was writing, answering the telephone and checking my email every time the red ball indicated a new message, I was losing something.

I realized this during the hour of silence that we priests of the Fraternity of St Charles Borromeo observe each day. In that hour we find the anchor of our lives. Silence is a serious necessity. While reading my breviary, I found that my eyes would fly quickly over the words, often without remembering anything a minute later. I read the texts of the Bible in the same way that I read my textbooks for the university, the same way I read the website of the *New York Times*, the same way that I watched *24*. I remained on the surface looking for the most important key words, or the most exciting scenes. Every pause, every breath, every conjunction, became an empty space I felt I had to eliminate. I was losing the capacity to contemplate and to read profoundly, and the capacity to be moved by the various shades of meaning. I was losing the perception of time as a positive experience.

□ □ □

The following year my superior asked me to help him as the vice rector of the seminary. From that moment on, I watched with growing interest the same dynamics that I was living, in the young men I had to educate. Educating them in the meaning of silence, for instance: 'When something you are reading strikes you, stop and contemplate it.' Telling them how to pray made me reflect on my own way of praying. I noted that some people watched films in their rooms on their laptops, which is frowned upon in the rule of our life – yet it had been my own obsession just a year before. Others maintained relationships with their families through SMS and telephone, but had weak relationships with their classmates. Some people wrote pages of emails, but were unable to finish their homework on time.

I saw myself in all these habits: what happens on a computer screen is almost always more attractive than what happens in a book, whatever it may be. An email always seems more urgent than anything else, and we check for them compulsively many times a day. It is like the anxiety I felt as an adolescent when the postman was about to pass us: would he bring a letter from *her*? Sometimes yes, sometimes no. Then the postman would leave, and only the next day could I be tempted to return to my window and wait. Today, I wait for much more banal messages with the same anxiety, and I waste a lot of time closing and opening the email program while I have other more important things to attend to.

Now, however, I also have an educational responsibility. This has helped me move out of the lethargy which I had fallen into, face my own problems and reflect seriously on those I sense in some of my seminarians.

□ □ □

3

THE PROBLEM

I realized there was a problem when I started to care for the fruit trees in our garden. I noticed that I had an unreasonable haste: I wanted the plants to grow more quickly, I wanted to have apricots in November and lemons in May. I wanted to get rid of the weeds once and for all – instead, they kept coming back again and again, after the fire, after the hoe, and even after spraying. I had to learn to *care* for the plants, and not try to solve all the problems in order then to move onto something else. I was treating the plants almost as if they were mechanical gadgets.

In reality, I saw the same dynamic at work in my educational duties. I noticed often that it was not possible to *solve* the problems my students had, and instead that it was necessary to *accompany* them, step by step, in an adventure which is extraordinary even when it does not lead to the hoped for result. With their speed, the technologies that filled my life were teaching me to be impatient. The 'efficiency above all' mentality that was taking root in me told me the only thing that matters is results. *But for results*, the lemon trees were teaching me, *we need time*.

It would be easy at this point to give in to nostalgic visions of the medieval age. So let me hurry to promise that I will not sing of a 1968 hippy utopia, forty years too late. Even if I was born in a 'back to the land' community, early on my family took another route. I am grateful to them for their sacrifices and the sense of realism which drove my parents to return to 'normality'. Still, I remain at times nostalgic for a bucolic life. But then what American isn't when he first sees Italy? How much beauty is hidden in every village centre! What vistas in Siena, or in proud Florence; and then the countless beautiful images of the Madonna painted by anonymous artists in every church in the countryside! It is enough for the eye to fall in love, and one asks how all this was possible back then.

Nevertheless, the problem of a nostalgic is that he does not live in the past. He lives today. How can we live today? This is the question that steadily grew within me. I am deeply convinced that I live for today – and not 'unfortunately so'.

It is not easy to find reasons for the experiences I described in the previous chapter. It does seem obvious that if we can do something in less time with less energy, then we should. It also seems obvious that the world in which we live cannot go back to being what it was fifty, a hundred, or a thousand years ago. And it is obvious that the people who still live as we did a hundred years ago are climbing over each other in order to be able to live the way we live today.

It is not obvious that a causal link exists between my work habits and my distraction in prayer. I was not able to clearly explain the difficulties that I was encountering, and in any case I kept living at 200 miles per hour. Every once in a while I had the doubt come to me that maybe all this efficiency was not bringing me any closer to the medieval and renaissance beauty that I love so much, that can nourish spirit and soul. But perhaps it was only some nostalgic fragment left over from my upbringing speaking to me. And in any case, if I said that over-reliance on technologies results in ignorance, or distraction, wouldn't that mean that I had become a determinist? Isn't it much more reasonable to say that tools in themselves are neither good nor bad?

In fact we often speak in this way, but it has never completely convinced me. I could no longer read with the same depth of a

few years before. I could quickly run my eyes over a lot of pages
and books, but the content did not really resonate with me. Is it
possible that this was just a question of using technological tools
in a better way – a moral problem? Or were they, too, to blame
for carrying me towards distraction?

Other things struck me: the cell phone had made communication more easy, but it had also invaded many places that up until
then had been special, almost magical: the church, the theatre,
the cinema, the train. How annoying it was to travel from Rome
to Milan with someone speaking loudly on their telephone, or out
of boredom, continuously changing their ringtone! And email,
which initially I used as a more secure way to send letters, and
which were very similar to those I used to write on paper, in just a
few years had become a commandment: 'Thou shalt respond
quickly!' After a few hours of waiting, I would start writing
another email like: 'Hi, I don't know if there was a problem with
the system, I don't know if you received the message I sent a few
hours ago this morning ...'.

Speed was the beauty of email, but it was also a noose around
my neck. I can't always and don't always want to respond quickly.
But I felt forced to do so – and I expected the same of my
correspondents. Is it really possible that we are simply all badly
educated, discourteous and 'immoral'? Or is there something
more profound going on here?

I read several philosophers who each sought, in one way or
another, to answer the problems that were emerging from my
observations. Some of them said that even the wheel had been a
terrible and marvellous revolution in human history, like the
printing press, gunpowder and the compass. Others said instead
that there is a substantial difference between our situation and
that of the revolutions of the bygone past: these are the people
who wonder if the atomic bomb is perhaps too great a power to
be responsibly managed by human beings. I asked myself: is there

a threshold beyond which knowledge and technical power exceed the human capacity to control them? From the first atom bomb to the present day, no one has been able to reach a definite conclusion on this question. In the end, it is nothing other than the drama the ancient Greeks recounted in the myth of Prometheus stealing fire from the gods. Without fire, it was very clear what the difference was between man and the gods. Prometheus' audacity brought fire – the power of technology – and thenceforth men raised themselves to the heights of the gods. Or the myth of Pandora, who out of curiosity opened the box, letting out powerful spirits which did not ever return. Her curiosity is similar to that of modern science, which investigates every aspect of the real. But knowledge is always ambivalent, carrying with it great riches and great dangers. This is exactly what we are living through with biotechnology, cloning and prenatal diagnosis. Is knowledge always a force for good? This is a difficult question, which the ancient Greeks understood in all its drama.

In my reading, I was attracted by thinkers and novelists who faced the problem of technology with equilibrium and with joy. There are not very many.[1] It is a theme which unfortunately is often talked of in near apocalyptic tones: for example, Lebedev, in Dostoevsky's *The Idiot* saw in the web of train tracks crossing Europe the third trumpet of the Book of Revelation; Thoreau saw in the telegraph a useless banality;[2] Theodore Kaczynski was opposed to the world of technology to such a point that he became a hermit and constructed bombs which he sent against leading economic figures of the time. There are the 'no global' movements or organizations, which periodically destroy our cities in the name of the simple life and brotherly love. Then there are films like Chaplin's *Modern Times,* or *L'ingorgo* (1978) by Luigi

Comencini, and an infinite number of other expressions providing a critique of the relationship between technology and humanity, but all of them find no joyful solution.

In his masterpiece, *The Lord of the Rings*, Tolkien places this intuition at the centre of the story. The ring which gives the title to the trilogy is a symbol of a power so great that no one is able to use it in a correct way, not even the most good and just characters. It tends to corrupt anyone. Along Frodo's path, many characters are attracted to the power which he has in his care; some want to attain it for themselves; others, who know of its power and danger seek to resist it, like the wise wizard Gandalf, or the beautiful queen of the elves, Galadriel. In the scene in which Frodo would like to get rid of the ring, giving it to the queen, she says:

> 'You will give me the Ring freely! In place of the Dark Lord you will set up a Queen. And I shall not be dark, but beautiful and terrible as the Morning and the Night! Fair as the Sea and the Sun and the Snow upon the Mountain! Dreadful as the Storm and the Lightning! Stronger than the foundations of the earth. All shall love me and despair.' She lifted up her hand and from the ring that she wore there issued a great light that illumined her alone and left all else dark. She stood before Frodo seeming now tall beyond measurement, and beautiful beyond enduring, terrible and worshipful. Then she let her hand fall, and the light faded, and suddenly she laughed again, and lo! she was shrunken: a slender elf-woman, clad in simple white, whose gentle voice was soft and sad. 'I pass the test,' she said. 'I will diminish, and go into the West, and remain Galadriel.'[3]

'She laughed again, and lo! she was shrunken': it is a beautiful description of one who looks power in the face, and chooses reality rather than indefinite possibility, present life rather than future evolution.

I am a Christian and I don't believe that my era is an age in which it is impossible to live well. It would be a lack of faith to believe that one can know God, love one's brother and live in peace only after having destroyed this or that 'structure of sin'.

When I discovered David Schindler's writings, I was immediately drawn to the positive vigour of his thought. For him, the fundamental problems are not the economic or social structures, but the logic which gives them form. The 'logic of love' is a reoccurring theme in his work, and remains a central theme in his most recent thesis, *Ordering Love*.[4] To improve the situation, we must refuse the fatalism which affirms the existence of an 'invisible hand' which guides the economy and physical evolution, we must stop believing in blind and inevitable progress, and place in the foreground the freedom of man, together with its highest expressions: love, friendship, beauty and sacrifice. I have a debt of gratitude to Schindler for having taught me a form of thought capable of breaking away from the usual clichés and constraints, and for having given me questions that have thrown new light on the problems of existence in our time.

Schindler also introduced me to the writings of Wendell Berry – to whom we shall soon return in more detail – a farmer and seminal writer in the panorama of American social thought. Initially he seemed to me an unreasonable utopian, but then he won me over with his novels replete with beautiful characters exhibiting human dynamics of every kind. He is not a dreamer after all: through his novels, I learned to look at my own life in a more light hearted way and at the same time in a deeper and more creatively critical manner.

Finally, I found an interesting train of thought in the neurological studies collected by Nicholas Carr in *The Shallows*, and in the book he quotes from most frequently, *The Brain that Changes Itself* by Norman Doidge. This book in particular proposed a peaceful starting point, rather than a contestable ideological one, to begin to understand the experiences I was having and which I observed in my students. Much has been written on technology on the basis of sociological and psychological studies. But at least for the layman they don't seem to lead to any clear conclusions. Some of them have demonstrated the wonderful educational capacity of television, and immediately there follows a demonstration of the opposite. The same is true for the cell phone (is it or is it not like a little microwave oven attached to your brain?), videogames (do they augment hand–eye coordination or do they diminish attention?), and so on. Many conclusions seem to be more determined by fear or self-interest, rather than by reason and data. Carr and Doidge instead have collected the most recent studies in neuroscience, which is finally able to explain some of the crucial mechanisms that can shed light on the relationship between technology and humans.

These writers underscore the central elements of my approach to the question of technology. But above all, my education as a physicist and my religious faith give me a profound trust in reality: I am convinced that reality does not betray us. The future can be intuited from past experiences. It cannot be known completely, but nor is it a leap in the dark. As a corollary to this, I am profoundly suspicious of schools of thought which do not recognize this or which underestimate the reality of evil, and erroneously believe in the infinite character of progress, in an unstoppable evolution, which will always proceed for the better. I know too well my own evil and that of other people, to believe this sort of myth.

I believe that what I do has a real effect on me and on those around me. I believe, therefore, that I have a real responsibility, especially in the lives of those I educate. And finally, I want to live this responsibility in a constructive and realistic way. I don't want to look for shortcuts to utopia. Nor do I wish to give up and accept mediocrity as if it were destiny.

I will start from the neurological data, in particular with regards to reading, in order to provide an easy foundation on which we can build. Then, I will describe some of the most important dynamics in new technologies. From those which are positive, such as the more simple modes of communication, and those less positive, like the dis-incarnation of human relationships. In the next section, I will speak of education: how can we face the problems I raise? I will describe my attempt at responding to this question and the form it is taking in my seminary. Finally, I propose a brief concluding sketch which collects the underground threads running through the book: the themes of power, love of reality and the joy of building homes for mankind.

II

□ □ □

NEURO-SURPRISES

Great is the power of memory, something terrifying, my God; a complex profundity, deep and infinite: and all this is spirit, and all this am I. What am I then, O God? What is my nature? Various, multiform life, immense.

St Augustine, *Confessions*, X, 17

4

□ □ □

THE TECHNOLOGY OF THE BOOK

I would like to start with a very ancient technology which will help us understand more recent innovations: writing. In this chapter and in the next, I base my arguments largely on the studies collected by Nicholas Carr in *The Shallows,* to which I refer the interested reader. His book has provoked wide debate, and I consider his principal argument, which shows a connection between our habit of reading and our capacity for thought, valid and pertinent.

But first, back to the beginning and a study of cuneiform and hieroglyphics. Both these forms of writing require memorization of hundreds of characters in order to be understood, not just the twenty-six that compose our alphabet. It isn't just a question of the difficulties inherent in a non-alphabetic language like Chinese. Even texts written using our own alphabet can be very hard to decipher, like the marble slabs used in Roman times. They are difficult to read because there are no spaces between the words. And what's more, there are many different abbreviations (it was hard work carving marble!) and there are no punctuation marks. Reading is difficult and it requires a lot of attention to recognize single words, let alone understand what they say. Texts were commonly read aloud, because the rhythm of the words helped in the understanding of its content. There is a famous passage in the *Confessions* of St Augustine where he marvels at the fact that St Ambrose could read in silence.

Then around the year 800, Irish monks began to introduce spaces between the words. And later, the invention of punctuation marks rendered the meaning and sense of the writing more clear and liberated intellectual capacities that could now be dedicated to understanding what was written, and not just the material act of reading itself. Therefore, it became physically easier to read in a quicker and more attentive way.

From all of this a powerful capacity for reflection arose. While one reads deeply, one also thinks and reflects more profoundly. One creates links in the memory, between what one is reading and has already experienced or what one has already thought. In this flux and reflux of ideas in memory, new and stronger links are created. Improvements in the technology of reading permitted the deepening of reflective capacity.

It is important to note another detail in this process: it takes a certain amount of time for information that has entered short term memory to be transferred into long term memory. If during this process the short term memory is filled with other data, the previous information is erased *without being transferred*. While reading a book, this is physiological: in a page of text there are some dense phrases and others that are less significant. Reading line after line, one can absorb the contents at the 'buffer' velocity of short term memory, while it is transferring into long term memory. One can also read more quickly by 'scanning' the page, but one does it with a different purpose. One does this like a hunter searching for data, and not like a contemplative immersing himself in the text. If I add other stimuli, filling the empty moments (for example, in a classroom when the professor is going on about material I think is irrelevant, I can write an email or read the headlines that are in the newspaper, or I can listen to music …), I tend to kick out of my short term memory the contents that it is receiving.

But is this really a problem? Distractions at times seem to augment our attention: this is the case of multitasking. To do more than one thing at a time is very simulating – it raises one's level of attention, and the body becomes one with the computer keyboard, or with the car while I am driving and speaking on the telephone. One can jump from one link to another, from one piece of information to another on Google, and not feel exhausted. The entire mind is intent on the search, and because it is stimulating it can even be enjoyable.

Nevertheless, this kind of attention is very different from 'deep reading', and tends to reduce the capacity for *concentration*. A series of articles in the *New York Times* on 6 June 2010 reported a similar finding: 'If you get used to having a broad attention span, you often then have a lot of trouble learning to be selective with it.' Carr says the same thing at the beginning of his book:

> I'm not thinking the way I used to think. I feel it most strongly when I'm reading. I used to find it easy to immerse myself in a book or a lengthy article. My mind would get caught up in the twists of the narrative or the turns of the argument, and I'd spend hours strolling through long stretches of prose. That's rarely the case anymore. Now my concentration starts to drift after a page or two. I get fidgety, lose the thread, begin looking for something else to do. I feel like I'm always dragging my wayward brain back to the text. The deep reading that used to come naturally has become a struggle.[1]

With that, Carr begins his series of neurological studies in order to understand what was happening to him.

The same phenomena can be observed in other places. If we take a quick look at the development of newspapers during the last fifty years, we can see that in general all readers today prefer short texts. Articles that just a few decades ago could be found in the daily papers are now only printed in the specialized journals. The general public no longer reads lengthy articles anymore. It is dramatic: just look at the first page of any national daily newspaper fifty years ago, to see how many long articles there were that the average reader could absorb. Or think of the famous debates between the two American candidates for President, Abraham Lincoln and Stephen Douglas in the presidential campaign of 1854. Douglas spoke for three hours and after Lincoln responded for four more! Who today could follow such a long chain of reasoning and respond immediately?

It is true that the human brain is naturally distracted. We are naturally attracted by movement, by things that change, and not by things that remain still. It is probably an evolutionary survival mechanism built into our brains. To learn the intense concentration necessary in order to read a book, and in particular a long book with detailed arguments, can require a lot of effort.

What is new and seems to be linked to the explosion in communication tools in the last half a century, is that the development of the brain does not necessarily proceed in the direction of an ever more refined capacity to reason and create connections between events and ideas. The process which began several thousand years ago with the invention of writing, and which has brought us a truly extraordinary capacity to concentrate, as opposed to the instinctive mechanisms attracted by movement, today seems to be favouring again primitive dynamics: those of a 'hunter'.

Maryanne Wolf affirms that 'The mysterious, invisible gift of time to think beyond is the reading brain's greatest achievement; these built-in milliseconds form the basis of our ability to propel knowledge, to ponder virtue, and to articulate what was once inexpressible – which when expressed, builds the next platform from which we dive below or soar above.'[2]

One of the studies Carr quotes that struck me the most was carried out in 2008. A video camera followed the eye movement of six thousand students of the 'net-generation', who grew up with the internet. The study revealed the great majority of subjects did not read in a linear way. The researchers were brought to the conclusion that 'digital immersion has even affected the way they absorb information. They don't necessarily read a page from left to right and from top to bottom. They might instead skip around, scanning for pertinent information of interest.'[3]

Another study that I found even more interesting, because it revealed a habit that I have, was done a few years earlier. In 2006 the web optimization guru Jacob Nielson did a study of people reading on the internet, in order to offer suggestions for web designers. A small video camera registered the eye movements of the 232 subjects while they read web pages of text and other content. He discovered that the eyes of nearly all of his subjects traced an 'F': two or three lines at the top of the page, and then a couple of half lines starting on the left, followed by a quick scan down the side of the page.[4]

In 1997 Linda Stone coined the phrase 'continuous partial attention', to indicate the state of fragmented attention created when we are divided between many different activities. She writes, 'Attention is the most powerful tool of the human spirit. We can enhance or augment our attention with practices like meditation and exercise, diffuse it with technologies like email and Blackberries, or alter it with pharmaceuticals. In the end, though, we are fully responsible for how we choose to use this extraordinary tool.'[5]

First of all we should recognize these dynamics, in order to reasonably judge the relationship between tools and users. In particular, as far as the internet, cell phones and multi-functional devices are concerned, we need to be conscious of the fact that they are structurally ordered to a type of reading that is superficial, a type of research which is more similar to hunting than to contemplation. It is true to say that the dichotomy between 'hunters' and 'farmers' goes back to the dawn of human history. But this is precisely the point: if it were not possible for the same person to be both a fast and efficient hunter, and an attentive and prudent farmer, which of the two abilities should be preferred?

5

□ □ □

READING AND WRITING

What makes this discourse particularly important is the fact that every experience that one has leaves a trace in the brain. I am speaking of neuroplasticity. The brain continuously adapts to the circumstances in which it lives, even on a physical level. Once it was thought the brain reached with physical maturity a substantially fixed form, and it worked more or less like a computer. Today we know that the reality is quite different. We know that neurons are continually born and continually die,[1] and form new connections between themselves. We were born with some neurological structures, but these structures can be profoundly modified by experience.

The meaning and importance of this discovery cannot be overestimated. One of the underlying dynamics is called Hebb's rule, formulated by the Canadian neuroscientist Donald Hebb in 1949: 'Cells that fire together wire together.' If two neurons more or less in the same area of the brain are stimulated at the same time by an experience, they can form physical connections between themselves and new dendrites grow. More recently Edward Todd and Michael Merzenich have demonstrated that there are other possible mechanisms. Not only does experience generate the neurological structures, strengthening and weakening the links between neurons, but it can also make entire groups of neurons change roles. Thus, for example, stroke victims can recover body movement by 'reprogramming' the neurons in an undamaged area, which then substitute for the damaged neurons. [2]

If an experience is repeated, it is easier on a physical level that the next similar experience be described by the same set of neurons. The same dynamic functions in the inverse: a repeated gesture, for instance, a tickle, is perceived as ever less strong the more it is repeated. [3] Every time that I experience a hand touching my belly that does not want to hurt me, my body reacts less strongly to the stimulus. At a cerebral level, the connections which at first sent a message to the muscles saying 'contract!', now do not send anything – and physically unnecessary connections are eliminated.

And that isn't all. It is sufficient that an experience be 'remembered' in order to strengthen the connections in play. A notable example of this phenomenon regards musical practice. One can practice by only *thinking* of playing, without actually touching the keyboard of a piano, and really improve. A study done in 1995 by Alvero Pascual-Leone demonstrated that a group of pianists who only imagined playing certain notes registered the same changes in their brains as others who actually played the keyboard! [4]

When new connections are created between neurons, they become the easiest route of communication. That is how habits are formed, both of action and of thought. All of this has deep links with our relationship with reality.

So let's go back to reading: deep meditative reading enriches our memory with real experiences. It forms our minds with rich and complex ideas. Reading the great classics of literature, we experience sentiments which perhaps in real life we have yet to encounter – but by reading them we experience them in such a concrete way that our brains are modified.

We become what we think, what we see, what we read, and what we do. This is not a mystical affirmation; on a neurological level, our experiences never leave us unchanged. They change us, for better and for worse, creating or strengthening new connections, weakening or eliminating others. Carr sums up the question in this way: 'Neuroplasticity provides the missing link to our understanding of how informational media and other intellectual technologies have exerted their influence over the development of civilization and helped to guide, at a biological level, the history of human consciousness.'[5]

We have seen that the technology of writing carries with it important consequences for our relationship with the world. For example, the invention of punctuation marks opened new possibilities of thought. The invention of hypertext links opened others. Some of these consequences are innocuous, some of them are positive and others less so. In particular, the structure of linear thought which has developed with the book, has become weaker, distracted these days by too many stimuli.

Linda Stone is an optimist. She thinks that we will learn to live with technologies with the same naturalness that we see with a musician and his instrument.

> With a musical instrument, it's awkward at first. All thumbs. Uncomfortable. Noise. With practice, instrument and musician become as one. Co-creating music. So it will be with personal technology. Now, a prosthetic of mind, it will become a prosthetic of being. A violinist with a violin. Us with our gadgets, embodied, attending as we choose.[6]

It is an interesting idea, but I don't think it sufficiently takes into account the fact that a relationship with an instrument is always bidirectional. A violinist can learn to collaborate with his instrument only at a high price. In his case, it is worth it: the negative consequences, on his mind and body (and on those who live with him!), of the thousands of hours necessary to practise in order to learn to play, are usually less important than the immense richness and beauty of his music. But he certainly does not learn that capacity for free. And it is interesting to note that different musical instruments require different amounts of time in order to be learned. After a few months of practice, a person can learn to play the guitar at least in a pleasing way; for the violin it takes years. And what if learning 'to play' our gadgets in an elegant way, as Linda Stone promises, took an even longer time? And what if not everyone was able, in the same way not everyone is able to learn to play the violin?

It is worth listening to what Stanislas Dehaene, a French neuroscientist says in a book which collects the fruits of his career as a student of reading: 'Behind the apparent diversity of human writing systems lies a core set of universal neuronal mechanisms that, like a watermark, reveal the constraints of human nature.'[7] As Dehaene notes elsewhere, speaking of the limits of human nature is not a 'right-wing' idea! Man has limits, which are difficult to describe in a general sense and apply to the whole human race, but which can easily be experienced in a single case. One of these limits is that the brain cannot optimize all processes. At a certain point, it has to choose. Let's take a closer look at our relationship with the instruments which we use to extend our capacities.

□ □ □

6

TOOLS ARE NOT NEUTRAL

The discovery of neuroplasticity helps us resolve an ancient philosophical problem regarding the nature of tools. Some say, as I alluded in the introduction, that a tool is simply at the disposition of its user: it is neutral, neither good nor bad. And there are others who say that tools are not neutral because they modify the relationship between a human and the world in a decisive way. Who is closer to being right? Let's take this step by step.

There is a big difference in saying technology is not neutral, and saying it is intrinsically evil. Here we need to make some clear distinctions. By 'neutral' we usually mean two things. First of all – taking it to the extreme – we mean that the internet was not invented by the devil. And even if there were a whiff of sulphur about it, since there are a lot of well meaning scientists and programmers involved, it cannot *only* be evil. If it is used badly, it is because men and women use it badly. So far, so good.

The problem is that here we tend to make an unjustified leap. That is, we tend to think, that since it is a 'neutral tool', only the user uses the technology. But this is not true: it is also the technology that 'uses' its user. Every tool has an impact on the person using it. Knowing what we now know about neuroplasticity, this affirmation no longer has the flavour of a vague philosophical opinion: it has to do with the growth and death, the strengthening and weakening of dendrites between neurons, and the reprogramming of groups of neurons for new functions.

Keeping all of this in mind, let us take a look at two of the instruments in the technological constellation surrounding our lives:

The *cellular phone*, or the 'elimination of space'. You can be reached anywhere. Remember when work relationships were generally circumscribed to the physical workplace? And calling you at home was only allowed at the gravest need? Now you can even work on the beach, and the result is that there is no longer any distinction between home and office. You can turn your phone off, but you cannot force everyone to do so. Thus you find yourself on the bus, in the theatre or in church, if not in your own office, quite often in the office of others. Space tends to become an indifferent scenography.

Certain experiences – the first school trip away from the family, university in a far away city – are no longer the same, since you can be reached at any time during any day, and the umbilical cord linking you to home is in many cases cut much later. Ever since there have been cell phones, appointments are taken in a very spontaneous manner – 'I'll call you when I am nearby'. Not all of this is evil, but nor is it neutral. These are profound changes in our way of understanding work, human relationships and our relationship with space.

Or take *television*, the possibility to choose the world in which you live. The availability of many channels makes it possible to continuously leap from one world to another (this is true of three or four channels, let alone the five hundred to be found on satellite TV). These instantaneous leaps have no precedent: not even the theatre of the absurd was ever able to create unlinked passages like anyone can with a remote control in hand. This experience strengthens within us the view that the world is not first 'given', but chosen. You want to feel something in particular? Then choose the program that will make you feel relaxed, excited, fearful, joyful, sentimental and so forth. Or you do not know what you want to feel, so you begin to zap through the channels, stopping for a few seconds on the images that most instinctively attract you.

Television has a complicated relationship with truth: it has the appearance of objectivity, but it is clear that it is easily manipulated. All you have to do is alter the point of view, the colours, the light, and all of a sudden everything changes. The detailed care for light and make-up, which are constantly present in television work, make the world inside the screen hyper-realistic, more real than the real world.

On this subject it is interesting to listen to what Neil Postman has to say. He is an American Jeremiah, a lamentful prophet. But like the Jeremiah of biblical memory, Postman too has a penetrating gaze and often hits the mark in his analysis of technological and communicative developments. *Technopoly* and *Amusing Ourselves to Death* are two classics that one can read in a few hours, but which leave an impression.

In the second book, he writes 'it is implausible to imagine that anyone like our twenty-seventh president, the multi-chinned, three-hundred-pound William Howard Taft, could be put forward as a presidential candidate in today's world. The shape of a man's body is largely irrelevant to the shape of his ideas when he is addressing a public in writing or on the radio or, for that matter, in smoke signals. But it is quite relevant on television. The grossness of a three-hundred-pound image, even a talking one, would easily overwhelm any logical or spiritual subtleties conveyed by speech. For on television, discourse is conducted largely through visual imagery, which is to say that television gives us a conversation in images, not words. [...] You cannot do political philosophy on television. Its form works against the content.'[1]

Marshall McLuhan, the father of the reflections on the media, and Postman's teacher, after a period in which he was put down as being pessimistic and deterministic, is coming back in style. Part of this renewed interest is due to the discovery of neuroplasticity, which offers a new explanation of the dynamics which he described decades ago. In *Understanding Media*, he bulldozes into the theme of the neutrality of tools:

> In accepting an honorary degree from the University of Notre Dame a few years ago, General David Sarnoff made this statement: 'We are too prone to make technological instruments the scapegoats for the sins of those who wield them. The products of modern science are not in themselves good or bad; it is the way they are used that determines their value.' That is the voice of the current somnambulism. [...] There is simply nothing in the Sarnoff statement that will bear scrutiny, for it ignores the nature of the medium, of any and all media, in true Narcissus style of one hypnotized by the amputation and extension of his own being in a new technical form. General Sarnoff went on to explain his attitude to the technology of print, saying that it was true that print caused much trash to circulate, but it had also disseminated the Bible and the thoughts of seers and philosophers. It has never occurred to General Sarnoff that any technology could do anything but *add* itself on to what we already are.[2]

Every technology carries with it a change in our approach and relationship with the world. This is precisely not neutral, since everything depends on *which* aspects of life are made easier and which ones are made more difficult, or impeded, like the perfume of lemons in an email.

□ □ □

7

EVOLUTION OF THE SPECIES

Of course, there are those who think that they can have it all. This is the case for Kevin Kelly. When he was young, he was a vagabond in search of the simple life in Thailand, and then he chose to become a collaborator for 'Whole Earth Catalogue'. From this moment on, he arrived through successive steps, thanks to his network of friendships, to be one of the principle contributors to one of the most important journals on technology, *Wired* magazine. Today, he is a fervent believer in the benevolence of technology. He speaks of it as the 'seventh kingdom' of creation, a necessary force that emanates from the spirit of man, and that carries us sometimes through painful moments but always towards a better future. In *What Technology Wants*,[1] he develops this evolutionistic theme over a lengthy 400 pages.

Unfortunately, it is a superficial thesis. Certainly it is suggestive to count the transistors in microprocessors, and to note that the quantity of transistors connected on the internet and in satellites spinning above our heads is similar to the number of neurons in the human brain. But if neuroscience teaches us anything, it is that the sheer number of neurons is not sufficient to generate the extraordinary flexibility of human thought.

He quickly dismisses the problem of 'power', that is, the question of whether the human brain is capable of governing what the human brain has created, and frequently uses as his guiding principle the idea that the more options there are, the better:

'More is better than less.' Technology offers more choices, and more ways to express ourselves: 'If we fail to enlarge the possibilities for other people, we diminish them, and that is unforgivable. Enlarging the scope of creativity for others, then, is an obligation. We enlarge others by enlarging the possibilities of the technium – by developing more technology and more convivial expressions of it.'[2]

The simple number of available choices, however, does not guarantee anything. Anyone who has ever looked for the right shampoo in the supermarket, or the right bolt in a hardware store, knows the frustration of a thousand choices, all of them wrong. The mechanisms that generated all these options are not only an attentive examination of the needs and desires of man, with functional and elegant solutions to them. Frequently we find ourselves in front of what *seems* to be an eloquent and economical solution, while in reality it is only an advertising gimmick. What I really desire is the *right* shampoo and the *right* bolt, not all the choices that I do not wish to choose from.

Perhaps unsurprisingly, Kelly says that 'without all of those choices, you could not find the right object you were looking for'. But this type of reasoning presupposes the evolutionary dynamic that he is forever keen to demonstrate: that the driving principle in the creation of new products and technologies is the 'survival of the fittest', and that a larger number of variations will bring us to the most adequate product for each user. I often, however, have had a different experience: books written to respond to a momentary desire in the market, which disappoint me for their poor quality and lack of lasting relevance; cell phones 'designed' to survive for just one year in my pocket. It seems to me that there is a lot more going on here than just blind evolution. I think that greed, deception, laziness and ignorance are also involved. Perhaps ignorance can be defeated by evolution, but not the other three.

Kelly ends his book with a prophetic vision, 'It will take all life and all minds and all technology to begin to see reality. It will take the whole technium, and that includes us, to discover the tools that are needed to surprise the world. Along the way we generate more options, more opportunities, more connection, more diversity, more unity, more thought, more beauty, and more problems. Those add up to more good, an infinite game worth playing. That's what technology wants.'[3]

This is an idea which can seem attractive, but it is an inadequate version of the facts. It is not a historical question, but a structural one. There exists a human nature, which has limits. We cannot keep all of the old and all of the new, something will be lost. And we should decide carefully precisely *what* to keep and *what* to lose.

□ □ □

8

EXCURSUS:
TECHNOLOGICAL PHENOMENOLOGY

This excursus is not a necessary part of the reasoning behind this book. So if it bores you please skip it and move on to the next chapter! However, I would like to offer these pages as a little example of the kind of thinking that can help us have a freer relationship with technology.

Video: television is interesting not only as a system of content but also as an object. Back-lit screens have a character that is completely different and almost magic with respect to every other object. They attract our eyes with a power that not even the great masters' oil paintings can command. What's more, they are totipotent, they can become any image: on the screen one can watch a comedy, the Pope celebrate the Way of the Cross on Good Friday or a porn flick. These are three experiences which more naturally would be more collocated in three very different places: the theatre, the church and the brothel, but which can live together in harmony on a living room television screen.

What's more, the screen is a one-way street, the watcher is a passive spectator. At least in the theatre you can throw rotten tomatoes! The sense of impotence one has in front of a television when the anchorman is giving bad political news, or the discourse of a liar, or the victory of a rival football team is impressive. One would like to participate, scream or do something, anything, but nothing is possible. The video camera brings me into the middle of an event with the same gesture with which it keeps me a million miles away from it.

I have had the occasion to work on a few video documentaries and it is worth noting the technique involved in video editing, which permits us to manipulate the world in a way which unlinks sound and images, and eliminates the downtimes which are the normal pauses in speech. On one occasion, after a long day of video editing I took a walk in downtown Bologna to relax. It was a very strange experience. It seemed like the cars were going too fast and I had to walk slowly in order not to become completely disoriented. When I heard people speak, there was so much information in their speech, in their gestures, in their eyes and in their words that I was not able to follow. Only a few days of work had made me used to seeing reality one frame at a time. While editing, I stopped the interviews 15 or 20 times to understand perfectly what people said. Then I cut out the boring parts and amplified the effect of the choice phrases with close-ups of the eyes and of the face. Reality, on the other hand, was chock full of information, content and stimuli, but it did not have the same rhythm as television.

Electric light: maybe it will make someone smile to see this in the list. But if we think about it, the instantaneity of the electric light is an experience that before our age was never possible. You push a button and *immediately* there is light. This sort of invention cannot be without consequences. Many things are made easier, you can read until late into the night, you can get up in the middle of the night without having to go search for matches and candles, you can walk in the city and be less afraid of thieves, and seen from far off the lights of a city are beautiful like terrestrial constellations (even though they have the cost of obscuring the celestial ones). But above all you can have light in the same instant in which you desire it. We should not underestimate this incredible power, which contradicts the law of every human activity up until Edison, *with the sweat of your brow you will earn your keep*. The instantaneity of electricity eliminates the annoyance of time lag between desire and satisfaction. Perhaps this was the beginning of the desire to have the world, and to have it now.

In more recent times the desire to have things instantaneously has entered other areas of life: instant communication, the telegraph, the telephone, the radio; buying and selling online with a credit card, online information updated in real time, live radio and television, Facebook and Twitter and so forth.

The clock: it has been widely recognized that the clock is one of the inventions which changed Europe and the rest of the world most profoundly. The clock imposes its own rhythm on time. It does not reflect natural rhythms, other than the time required for 32,768 oscillations of a quartz crystal, which has been defined as a 'second'. For this reason, time as we have defined it requires bi-annual corrections – daylight saving time – and it imposes an abstract quantity of time to the working day. Instead of working when there is work to do and resting when there isn't, we remain in the office for eight hours (in the best of cases). It is interesting to juxtapose on this rhythm the natural rhythm of light and shadow, imposed by nature, because the human body participates in the rhythm of the seasons. This is most easily noted in the places where darkness remains longer, in the higher latitudes. There, it is a surprise to no one that obeying the clock and not the light generates health complications.

The clock has also given origin to a new religion: *taylorism*. The cult of efficiency. Beyond the extremes denounced by films such as Chaplin's *Modern Times* (1936), and innumerable other works of art, it seems that taylorism has penetrated into the most elementary aspects of our daily lives. A friend of mine told me that when he needed to find a mechanic, he found one much more quickly using Google. I said it was true, but asked: why did you need to find him so quickly? I tried to underline that he was using efficiency as his most important criterion, without asking himself what was the cost of that speed. For example, what are the criteria by which mechanics are listed on Google? Did you really gain anything doing everything alone, and not asking for help from another human being? Who do you trust? What happens to a society in which everyone wants to do everything without asking for help? And why are we happier to trust strangers and algorithms, than friends? Do we know what we are paying to have everything right away?

Skype: the best thing about voice over internet protocol (VOIP) programs is that you can have free telephone calls. That of course is not to be underestimated. It is a phenomenon that makes even the biggest telecommunications companies tremble. And it can make for significant savings for the user: the small business, the missionary fraternity, the college student. There is, however, another factor that is interesting. Not paying for the telephone call tends to make us think that time is free too, while time is the most scarce commodity of all. When I can't phone using VOIP, I notice that I give a different value to the conversation. I have to make a clear decision: speaking to this person is so important I am willing to pay for it.

On Skype we can even see each other, and with dear friends this can be a richer experience than just an audio telephone call. I find, however, that it is also a more frustrating experience because you cannot look each other in the eye. There is at present no way

to make the video camera coincide with the image of the face of
the other person. You can pretend, by staring at the camera in
order to give the other person the impression that you are looking
directly at them. But it is forced. Not being able to see the other
does not bother me in a normal telephone call, nor when I
communicate through letters. And finally when I am in front of a
camera I feel like I am on a stage, to an extent I never feel when I
stand in front of those same people in reality.

Digital: what are we talking about when we talk about *digital*? It is
in general a series of methods which permit us to translate an
analogical phenomenon made of infinite variations into a
sequence of only two elements: 1 and 0, 'on and off'. If we think
about it, it is incredible that a sound can be represented very
faithfully through digital processing. A sound is infinitely variable,
even if it is a very simple dynamic, one dimensional, because it is
'just' compression and rarefaction of air. Only one variable, the
pressure of air, is able to transmit the incredible richness of a
symphony, the absolutely unique voice of the beloved, the sum-
mery sound of a cicada. And wonder of wonders, that single
variable can transmit all these sounds simultaneously, and I can
distinguish them, the horn from the violin, the singer from the
cicada!

   This is not the place to go into depth regarding the mystery of
music. I was speaking of digital, of the conversion of the richness
of sounds into bits, 1 and 0. We use a mathematical procedure
invented by Fourier, which permits us to give an approximation
of any curve. This permits the pressure of air at any given instant
to be approximated with a sequence of simple functions which
can be generated in a mechanical way, up to any desired level of
precision.

   If I want to put this curve on a CD, I have to first convert the
analogical signal into a sequence of bits. To do that, I use Fourier's

technique. If I am working at CD quality, that means 44,100 hz. I am therefore measuring the height of the curve and I register its value 44,100 times each second. That is in effect a very good approximation, and if the recording is well done the CD can be quite satisfactory. But even at this level of precision, I am losing information. Everything that happens in between the moments in which I measure is lost. The approximate curve will then be interpreted by the CD reader, and translated into pressure in the air through a loudspeaker.

All of this is more complicated in the case of images. In order to be converted into a digital format, an image has to be translated into pixels. That is, into a series of points in which the quantity and colour of light is measured. They are discreet, separated points that have no connection one with the other. Each of them has a colour and intensity value which can be converted into numbers, in the same way we do with music.

It is similar to the cross stitching that my grandmother used to do, a cloth grid in which each box was filled with a little cross of coloured yarn, forming an image. Certainly the cameras and the screens we currently use are much more sophisticated than those that we had just few years ago. And they do permit a wonderful approximation of an image. But we can clearly see the limits in this process. A screen made of pixels ordered in parallel lines makes it easier to reproduce vertical or straight lines. But if we use just a simple curve, that image is no longer so beautiful. In fact you can show a curved line only through approximation by small vertical and horizontal lines.

Let's take the black and white text that I am seeing as I write this page. Here is an enlarged image of the page.

The programmers use a very refined system to convince my eyes that I am looking at curved forms of the Cambria font. But in reality, I am looking at a screen made of chequerboard pixels

ssimazione delle
schermo fatto di
tte lungo le assi (
ù tanto bella, pe

illumined by differing intensity and colour. What do they do? They use grey, red and blue tonalities in order to convince my eyes that the legs of the 'N' are thinned out or the leg of the 'p' makes an elegant curve where it connects with the circle. If we then look at a page in a well-printed book, we can immediately see the difference between digital and analogical printing. Digital produces, within its chequer-board of possibilities, a more or less good copy; analogical is a thing in itself. Digital is structurally incapable of shades of meaning, it has to atomize the world into little fragments, even if perhaps with a resolution that is beyond the limits of human perception, in order to measure them and recompose them in another place. But what emerges does not have the density of a single musical note, or a single brushstroke of colour, in its complex unity.

Without going deeper into the issue, I would like to note that this approximation of the world contains a powerful and hidden ontology. Digital pretends that things can be decomposed into the elements 1 and 0, at least up to a resolution you can perceive. Even more weighty are the consequences of the fact that digitalization treats the world as a thing that can be replicated an arbitrary number of times, since it is only a sequence of bits. You can copy CDs, movies or programs without losing any information. This creates an experience of the world that is radically opposed to the experience of unrepeatable things localized *here* and nowhere else. Digital tends to make us experience the world as something generic, which is everywhere the same.

III

□ □ □

THE OBSTINACY OF
THE PHYSICAL

*I have never been so
attached to life.*

Ungaretti, *Veglia*

In the third part of this book, I would like to offer a series of reflections about the technological mediation of human relationships. I write these pages in an unsystematic form. They are incomplete, a work in progress. I wish I were able to write a textbook, but at the moment I am unable to do so. My neurons are burned out by too much multi-tasking! I cannot write more than two pages in a row, let alone work through the details of a complex argument, or consider fully the relationship between technology, man and society. Perhaps, however, these limitations will make these pages more useful as a reflection of our times.

We are in a time of extremely rapid change, where tools are invented and then become obsolete before being adequately understood. What I would like to do is to recall some of the experiences that we all have, and in light of these experiences pose a few questions. I don't have any claim to completeness, nor can I preach from a podium. I am too mixed up with the problems I describe. Unfortunately, I won't be able to avoid some generalizations. These generalizations seem acceptable to me only because my primary objective is not to offer a detailed interpretation of every aspect of technology. Rather, I wish only to remind you, gentle reader, of the obstinate nature of physical reality, and some of its consequences.

☐ ☐ ☐

9

THE BEAUTY OF TECHNOLOGY

Every month, all the members of the Missionary Fraternity I belong to meet together to speak of the most important events that happened during the last month. We tell of the miracles we see, the most interesting encounters we have had, the changes that have happened in us. We ask questions too: How to teach better? How to face the sickness or death of our dear friends? What does a natural disaster teach us? We speak of beauty, pain, love and suffering, of life. It is a very meaningful occasion which we consider the central moment of our common life together.

Our Fraternity today is present on four continents, and has more than one hundred members. We see each other infrequently, usually only once every two years for a week long summer vacation. About ten years ago, we felt the need for greater cohesion; we asked ourselves: how can we make the unity of the fraternity grow? And so we had the idea to turn our monthly house meeting into a worldwide teleconference. All of the houses connect, and what each person says can be heard by all. At the beginning of the meeting the secretary calls roll: 'Siberia?', 'Yes, we are here!' 'Washington?', 'Present!' 'Madrid?', 'Hello to everybody!' I vividly remember the joy of the first roll call in real time through all the faces, all the personalities, all the cities. It gives us what was and remains an extremely strong feeling of unity, adventure, and delight, that we are truly one thing. 'We live far away as if we lived together forever', says our founder. That is exactly how it is.

This monthly occasion is one of the most looked-forward to in our lives. I believe it would be more difficult for most of us without this support. And when I think of Francis Xavier, who had to wait for two years to receive a response to one of his letters – if the ship that carried the precious text did not run aground – I am even more grateful.

There are many other things that make me give thanks. One of our current missionaries in Taiwan became aware of our Fraternity by reading some of the missionary letters we publish on our website. How many years would he have had to wait in the little country village where he lived before one of our missionaries passed through, if he had not had access to the internet?

Or again, I think of the production of our videos that certainly would not have been possible even just a few years ago. Today, with very little money, we are able to create beautiful and articulate documentary videos to communicate the newness of Christian life. I have participated in the creation of four of these videos, and I am happy to have been able to work on these projects. I have seen how video as a medium of communication can open people's hearts. Through these projects I have also been enriched by the lives of people who I will probably never meet, but who have become dear to me, and who nourish my imagination and my faith.

For the last few years I have been trying to publish religious books in America and in several European countries. When I saw in the newspapers that the annual Frankfurt book fair was about to begin, I had the idea to go and try to meet some of the editors face to face. With so little time to get ready, what could I do to prepare for the trip? Use the internet, of course (iMac, I love you!). So I went onto the book fair website to see which publishers would be there and which of them would be interested in books of the sort we write, leaping about from site to site to find the best fit. And last of all I bought a plane ticket on e-Dreams, booked a hotel on Hotels.com, and set off.

□ □ □

10

IRREPRODUCIBILITY

I recently received an email from a friend of mine named Anna. She wrote to me of a particularly dramatic day upon which she discovered the friendship of a person to her very dear. The letter was beautiful, a simple and moving story. Then, a few weeks later I was speaking with a mutual friend about this message, and she revealed she too had received the same email. But wasn't it an email sent to *me*? Or was it copied for ease and sent to several people? And then, why do we tend to feel disappointed when we discover this sort of thing? Why should the letter be less valuable if it was sent to others as well?

The same thing is true for works of art. At Christie's auction house, originals are worth millions, and reproductions, even when they are not distinguishable to the buyer, are worth no more than a few thousand euros. Also, when an artist makes several copies of a work, like in the case of prints and woodcuts, he or she numbers them. It is not the same thing to have an original or a copy. It is not the same thing to have an original or number 53 out of 100.

Walter Benjamin writes, and I paraphrase, 'even in the case of highly perfect reproduction, one element is still missing: the *hic et nunc* of the work of art – its unique and unrepeatable existence in the place in which it is displayed. [...] The technique of reproduction, perhaps we could say it thus, takes the reproduction outside the realm of tradition. By multiplying the reproductions, technique places a quantitative series of events in the place of a unique event.'[1]

What changes in the case of a personal letter? The valuation of the person changes. My friend wrote a message which, in order to save time, she sent to others. In this communication the message was taken out of the intimate context of a friendship between sender and receiver. What predominated was the material, pure and simple, not the complicated web of intention, form and content which exists inside an unrepeatable and personal context. One sign of the falseness of this action is the sense of guilt it creates, which can be found in the fact that the sender tends to hide the fact that it was a message sent to several people. For example, Christmas cards are often signed by hand, even if the rest is pre-printed. (Dear Anna, don't be angry with me, I am much worse than you. I respond to your carbon copy letter with a book!)

I know a lot of people, and I am among them, who want to be esteemed above the level they deserve. Take Facebook profile photos: most don't necessarily reflect what a person really *is*, but rather what he or she would like to *seem*. It is a small and absolutely pardonable vanity, but it unveils a way of being that eats away at friendship. Through these little insincerities comes a mentality in which power is more important than truth. But what does all this have to do with Web 2.0? On blogs or social networks, each person is an emitter of information, and most messages are sent out into the ether to a plurality of receivers. This is something different than a conversation among friends. In an essay-letter written to Facebook (as though it were a person), Adam Briggle faces this problem of mass communication:

> Because of the mixed audience potentially viewing these public expressions [...] I do not feel all that free. In fact, I

begin to sympathize with the mass media broadcasting cor-
porations that have to produce content suitable for everyone. In these spaces, I am not playing with my identity or
expressing myself so much as trying to purify a neutral self
suitable for broadcasting to the viewing mass. It is the art of
self-censorship in an attempt to handle the collision of life
contexts that normally remain separate. I have seen innocent
comments spin out a thread of rancour, because what is best
said to one is best said otherwise to another and not at all to
a third.'[2]

Seen from one's own point this may not be very convincing. 'All
right, virtual communities may not be as strong as real ones, but
does it really matter?' It is easier to understand if we look at it
from the point of view of the receiver. Even if I write carbon copy
messages or books to save time, I would prefer that my friends
write to me as an individual on a private, one to one basis. I would
like to have our conversation happen with a balanced rhythm
between speaking and listening. I would like our friendship to be
full of sincere charity. Exactly what I do to others almost without
thinking, I wouldn't want to be done to me.

When I go onto an internet forum to try and solve a problem
with my computer, I can rapidly access the conflated knowledge
of many thousands of people. And I am often able to find a
solution quickly, but I tend to reduce these people to mere givers
of information, which is something less than persons. On the
other hand, I would not like to be treated as a simple giver of
information but as an unrepeatable being. I am not a mere event
among events. I am not a mere function among functions, or a
drop in the ocean. The concept of *personhood*, of which the
Christian West is justly proud, affirms that every man and woman
is a whole, an infinite. I am a unique event, and I find in the
unrepeatability of the flesh and of local human relationships, the
in-eliminable base for the strong and lively friendships that I seek.

□ □ □

11

SPIRIT AND BODY

I did not always have a strong appreciation for the physicality of human relationships. Once upon a time I was more attracted to the icy solitude of Descartes. But ten years in Italy, with very good teachers, have taught me to profoundly enjoy the perfume of a magnolia (which reminds me of the lemon and honey teas of my childhood), and to exult at the taste of a steak together with a '97 Brunello. During the evenings in which we sing folksongs in my seminary, I learned the beauty of spending time together. Sometimes I still feel the old desire for the philosopher's solitude, or I wish I had some mask to protect me, but I no longer doubt that letters, telephone calls and SMS cannot substitute direct human relationships.

I remember in elementary school we used to pass love notes between students. They were ridiculous for how direct they were. I think I once wrote to a girl: 'Would you like to be my girl-friend?', with two boxes to check, 'Yes' and 'No'. In high school things were more complicated and I usually did not have the guts to ask the question in person, so I tried on the phone. I was there straining to the utmost to interpret the microseconds of each pause and the tones of the voice, in order to understand the real intentions of my friend. I remember that certain relationships were in a sense doubled: there was the telephone relationship and the relationship in person during school. Rivers of words which we said in the evening did not seem to survive the light of the next day.

When I finally had a girlfriend for real, I immediately realized that being together was completely different from these interminable telephone conversations. In the first place it was much more difficult to mask my feelings. When I was tired, or tired of sweet words, I could not hide behind some monosyllable pronounced here or there on the phone. I was all of one piece, readable every instant and not only when I came out of my silence. The look in my eyes said more than many words. The caresses I so deeply desired were a sign of love, but they quickly became empty and we felt the need to find words ever stronger and gestures ever more daring, to say the same emotion. How strange it is, and how clumsy you feel, when you understand that an excess of expression stifles love!

This is significant because it helps us to understand that the language of love, like other languages and other fundamental human experiences, is infinitely variable and requires all the senses and all the expressive registers, even just to approach from far off that which we would like it to express. It helps us to intuit that every communication that does not include the physical presence of people, but is presented only with words, images and sounds mediated through a machine, loses the greater part of its effectiveness. After all a word written in a text message isn't anything except a word even if accompanied by a smiley. It does not have the individuality of a word written by hand, which betrays the haste or the care, as well as the personality, of the person writing. A word said on the telephone says more, but it can also be the result of a fiction. The language of love, like the language of religion, needs personal and bodily communication. You can trust a person, not a message. You can entrust yourself to a person and follow him, love him.

I can feel a leaping in my heart for someone who is here now with me. I can see her face, evaluate the sincerity of her smile, the purity of her gaze. I can shake her hand and measure the amount of her conviction, and of her human warmth. Of course, all of this can be falsified too, but there is no alternative. And it is much easier to fake it on the telephone, or by email.

In my body I experience the beauty of relationships, of which the physical limits are not a mortal shell, but a permeable boundary that permits communion. Precisely because my hand is not the same as that of the person who is shaking it, it is beautiful that our two hands be united. If there were no boundary, nor could there be the surprise and gratitude that we experience for the nearness of another. We would be one, but not in the rich and fathomless way Jesus means in chapter 17 of the Gospel of John. It would rather be the night in which all cows are black, in which being and nothingness are indistinguishable.

In the flesh there is less confusion. First of all because there is a certain sense of modesty in front of a physical presence, which helps to not rush, to not demand the fusion of our souls on the first date. And in the meantime, thanks to the continual corporeal messages which arrive through gestures, tone of voice, facial expressions, pauses and so forth, we get an idea of the other person without having to bring everything out into the forced clarity and typical impoverishment of direct discourse. Tip-toeing around certain themes is not necessarily a lack of love for the truth. It can very well express respect for the freedom and subtlety of certain truths. Some themes are like the cyclamen which can only live under the shadows of the trees in the woods. Direct light kills them.

12

☐ ☐ ☐

THE INCARNATION IN THE AGE
OF FACEBOOK

The college kids I know often say to one another, 'See you tonight on Facebook,' and they chat from their bedrooms more willingly than they go out and have a beer together. What does it mean when human relationships are lived through a screen rather than in person? 'Listening to a CD is like going to bed with a photo of Bridget Bardot,' said the famous orchestra conductor Sergiu Celibidache. Something is lost in the translation from live to a disk, something vital. The same is true for other types of mediation like Facebook.

What is Facebook? It is an example of the social networks that for the past few years have been popping up like mushrooms everywhere. In some sense it is a village square which permits people to meet, put up window displays about themselves and their lives, and stay in touch. And in fact everyone, from the Pope to the founder of Facebook, Mark Zuckerberg, says that social networks respond to a very deep desire that we all have, the desire for communion. But let us take a look at how they interpret that desire:

Meeting each other. If we accept that a person is body and soul, we should recognize that there is something fundamentally different between a virtual meeting and a real meeting in the flesh. To smell a scent of perfume, to shake a hand, give a kiss or look each other in the eyes, laugh together (not type *hahahahaha*)… All of this is possible only in the flesh.

So if I am worried about a phrase like 'see you on Facebook' or that people are happier to chat in their rooms than to go out and have a beer together, it is because this radically alters the meaning of being together. This kind of vicarious relationship, in solitude, is to direct relationships what pornography is to marital relations.

Putting up window displays about one's life. From time immemorial people have been tempted to wear masks. People want to make known certain aspects of themselves and conceal others. This posture is inevitably brought to light precisely in relationships with friends, because it is impossible to hide the truth about yourself for long with close friends. Being without a mask in front of another person is the essence of a mature human relationship. Everything else is just 'public relations'.

So what happens when two, three, four hours a day (or 'always', as some cell phone companies have been recently advertising), you live in a virtual world with a face that you constructed yourself? What happens when the public 'I' becomes more important than the private 'I'? Is it possible for a person to live under the gaze of the entire world?

Keep in touch. The human person made in the image and likeness of the One and Triune God is made for communion. This explains the extraordinary growth of Facebook, which interprets this ultimate desire. But what does Facebook do with it? Friends become a quantity, 'I have 731 friends …'. Close friends, simple acquaintances, and ex-girlfriends are all on the same level. Oh, yes: the ex-girlfriends. You need courage to go up to your ex and speak to her. You have to be clear, you have to know what you want. Sending her an SMS is already a little easier, and keeping in touch on Facebook is really easy, in the solitude of your bedroom, not really in the presence of anyone, without any meaningful looks, pauses or facial expressions which reveal the sentiments the other is feeling. In solitude, you can write without really meaning it: 'You know, I was thinking of you, maybe we could see each other …' Hell, as far as I can imagine, must be something similar. A terrible solitude of masks without anything behind them, without ever the joy of true communion. That joy which Tarkovsky speaks of, when one of his characters in *Andrei Rublev* says, 'You're tired and you cannot take it anymore. And all of a sudden you meet in a crowd the gaze of someone, a human gaze, and all of a sudden everything becomes simpler.'

13

□ □ □

PORNIFIED

In the last few years dozens of books have come out about the porn epidemic which is becoming evident all throughout the world. These include Pamela Paul's, *Pornified*; in the realm of psychology, *Clinical Management of Sex Addiction* (2002), edited by Patrick Carnes and Kenneth Adams, which contains articles published in specialized journals of previous years; while others have tried to take into account recent developments in neuroscience such as *Wired for Intimacy. How Pornography Hijacks the Male Brain*, or *The Drug of the New Millennium: The Brain Science Behind Internet Pornography*. Meanwhile, some are personal testimonies, one of the most interesting being *Porn Nation* by Michael Leahy.

Leahy's book says that nearly 60 per cent of web traffic is pornography; of course this number is put into question because there is no consensus on the unit of measurement (megabytes? webpage visits? key words searched for?). But the economic gains generated by selling pornography speak for themselves. In 2006, the year Pamela Paul's book came out, the pornography industry generated something like 97 billion dollars in sales: more than Microsoft, Google, Amazon, eBay, Yahoo, Apple, and Netflix put together.[1] Even if the details remain very unclear, it is obvious that this is a phenomenon of huge dimensions and great importance. Precisely our materialistic culture seems to be galloping towards the most extreme dematerialization – after having reduced the infinite beauty of loving relationships to a pure physical mechanism, we are decomposing them into the banal virtuality of a group of pixels on a back-lit screen.

I do not mean to go into detail on this theme here. I only want to insist we consider this: the phenomenon of pornography as a form of addiction. Psychiatrist Norman Doidge, in his extraordinary book *The Brain that Changes Itself* makes this claim. He speaks from his experience as a doctor, giving examples from some of his patients. He then makes the link with neuroplasticity: you cannot look at pornographic images, which stimulate the production of large quantities of neurotransmitters, and remain the same. Your very brain is modified as in other addictions:

> The addictiveness of Internet pornography is not a metaphor. Not all addictions are to drugs or alcohol. People can be seriously addicted to gambling, even to running. All addicts show a loss of control of the activity, compulsively seek it out despite negative consequences, develop tolerance so that they need higher and higher levels of stimulation for satisfaction, and experience withdrawal if they can't consummate the addictive act. All addiction involves long-term, sometimes lifelong, neuroplastic change in the brain. [...] The men at their computers looking at porn were uncannily like the rats in the cages of the NIH, pressing the bar to get a shot of dopamine or its equivalent. Though they didn't know it, they had been seduced into pornographic training sessions that met all the conditions required for plastic change of brain maps. Since neurons that fire together wire together, these men got massive amounts of practice wiring these images into the pleasure centers of the brain, with the rapt attention necessary for plastic change.[2]

These results are also confirmed by the work of Federico Tonioni, a psychiatrist who in November 2009 opened the first public clinic in Italy to cure internet addictions, at the Gemelli hospital in Rome:

In my work I noticed basic changes in the way of thinking, in my interviews with drug addicted patients. It was if something structural had changed on the level of their minds, and in particular in young addicts. So we started a pilot project, a clinic for internet dependence. It provoked an enormous resonance with the media. Out of that experience we identified five types of addiction: online pornography; online gambling; information overload, the ceaseless searching for useless information; social networks; and role-playing games. And we also noticed that there are two different types of patients: the over-30 group, who are generally addicted to pornography and online gambling, and have a compulsive approach linked to a behaviour addiction. They remind me a lot of cocaine addicts or bulimics. Then there is the second group of patients, which are of a larger number, that are at first completely unaware of having an addiction. They are all young people accompanied by their parents. From the point of view of this clinic, the numerically most significant problem today are role-playing games, but there are a lot of unidentified problems with respect to social networks, chatting, etc. I know many people who participate in the same blog with three or four different profiles, one authentic with the real name, and others with other names to make users of the blog argue among themselves. Then, after a while, the real user makes peace between his fake profiles in order to play the hero! It is a tendency which is present in real life too, but which on the web finds the concrete possibility of actually happening. It's very hard to turn back, once you have had certain experiences.[3]

These are dark and disquieting thoughts. The internet is a drug?! One thing is at least clear: there is a real problem, and it is growing, according to those who engage with it directly. Consider that a relatively innocuous drug like alcohol can create painful addictions which are hard to heal. Those who have had the greatest success caring for alcoholics, the various groups that grew out of the Alcoholics Anonymous twelve-step program, base a lot of their approach on mutually sustaining human relationships (buddy programs), and the elimination of temptation from the places where people live and work. But what would they do if alcohol were freely available 24 hours a day from every gadget in the house, from the cell phone to the computer?

□ □ □

14

THE MIND OF GOD

In the beginning, the internet seemed like a wonderful opportunity to play hide and seek: instead of being myself I could be anyone I wanted. I could hide behind one or more avatars, I could pretend to be someone completely different from the person I am in reality. It was said that everyone would begin to act as they would like to, as if there were no rules or social norms.

This is not exactly true. On the one hand, anonymity as such does not reveal itself as being particularly useful. Many psychologists note that some pathologies become worse if the patient hides in anonymity. On the other hand, there are many technical ways to identify the single user notwithstanding his attempt to conceal himself. In the last few years these means have become very powerful. What we do on the internet is registered in many places, and it is ever easier to recompose the mosaic and identify the user.

Traces are left on local servers, on internet providers and every site that we visit. In many countries a service provider is required to conserve for years a record of every single site visited by each user. These archives are obviously backed up and can easily be made accessible for a period of time much greater than that provided by law. An archive of our actions is also found in our own computers, in the browser cache. If these details are not erased, some of the data (so-called 'cookies') can trace a user even when he does not log in. Then there are the archives of Google, and other search engines: the 'web history' of Google accounts makes it possible to record every activity on the internet and consult it years later. (This web history service is activated by default on every Google account ...) Nearly every site contains an archive of its own visitors, which can be identified through the IP address of the computer that connected to it.

Why are all these archives kept? One reason is to protect oneself in case of police searches, in order to be able to demonstrate that you are not guilty of having visited an illegal site. Another reason is worth a lot more money. Google remembers all of the actions of its users (and with most of the latest browsers, including Firefox, Chrome and Safari, we are all 'Google users' through the 'safe browsing service'), because information is the main secret of its success. Having a lot of information on the real use of the internet means being able to optimize searches. It also means being able to send relevant advertising to each user. Already Google reads all of the emails that travel through Gmail to be able to place ads that are interesting to each user. And evermore they try to identify the single user, even when he or she uses different computers, to be able to send advertising that meets his taste. To get an idea of the dimensions of the phenomenon we are talking about, just observe that in 2009 Google sold something like 23 billion euros in advertising alone.

What is disquieting is that these records are never eliminated. Anybody who has tried to eliminate false news from the internet, or ideas that one no longer holds, old posts on a blog, knows that it is not easy. Often it is impossible. Add to that a lot of information, books bought, sites visited, comments written on Facebook, and you have a huge pile of acts from which it seems impossible to ever distance oneself.

This is something like the mind of God: everything that you ever did is recorded. But with one important difference: with Him, it is possible to ask for and receive forgiveness and erase the memory of sin. God's memory is perfect, but it is also merciful. God is not the 'accuser', he who remembers every detail in order to use it against us.

So what should we say about privacy? It seems to me to already be a topic that is out of date. There are so many ways to spy on internet use, and it is worth so much money to do so that I don't think it is a technique that will disappear in the short term. And in a sense, it does not seem like a problem because it re-establishes the theme of responsibility in an area which originally seemed to have eliminated it. You want to do something wrong or something you would be ashamed of doing if someone else knew it? It used to be possible just to make a fake email account and voilà – unlimited freedom, without consequences. That you can't do that so readily today is not so great a loss.

Then again, is it possible for people to live without committing errors? And if we commit them, is it right that we can never be freed from them? In the current political climate, in which the past of every candidate is examined with a microscope to search for tools against their candidacy, the problem of privacy seems an important one only for people in the public eye. But let us not forget that it is now an ordinary practice to do an internet background check on candidates for a job or for a research position.

What would happen if our governments changed? That does not seem to me to be an alarmist question. The twentieth century was full of rapid political changes. There is no reason to think that they cannot repeat themselves. I say all this not to raise the spectre of a conspiracy theory but to remind us that there is a serious issue which has not yet been tackled satisfactorily.

How can we defend our right to not be slandered? How can we repair the damage when it happens? How can we offer new life to those who have made mistakes, and not be resigned that they be irremediably weighed down by their past? I make more mistakes every day than I can count. Sometimes I hurt the people I love, besides those I simply tolerate. I really need to be forgiven. If this forgiveness were not possible, if every one of my acts should remain fixed forever without appeal, I could only despair.

I don't have a technical solution to suggest. I can only say that to me it seems inhuman to record every act, if we are then not also able to forgive and fix wrong doings.

□ □ □

15

CREATIVITY AND COLLECTIVIZATION

Jaron Lanier is one of the true pioneers of the internet, among the inventors of virtual reality, and a famous writer for *Wired*. Today he is one of the most important critics of Web 2.0, in particular in his latest book *You are not a Gadget*.

In an interview with Gianni Rotta for the *Sole 24 Ore* (10 October 2010), he said:

> In the time of the internet revolution, my collaborators and I were always laughed at because we foresaw that the web would be able to give free expression to millions of individuals. 'Come on', they told us, 'people like to watch TV and not be in front of the computer.' When the revolution happened though, creativity was killed and the web lost its intellectual dignity. If you want to know something you ask Google, which sends you to Wikipedia, and that's it. Otherwise people end up in the extremist sites, where they listen only to the people who confirm their ideas. [...] It is obvious that a collective chorus can't write history, nor can we entrust public opinion to the loud mouth extremists on the blogs. The mass has the power to distort history, damaging minorities, and the insults of online flamers that ossify the debate and disperse reason.

Lanier's is a voice worth listening to because it speaks from the heart of the technological world and not from a log cabin in the forest. He is not a reactionary but a creative man who considers the effect of collective work, for example Wikipedia.

In an interview in which he presents his books on Amazon.com, he says that:

> Collectives have a power to distort history in a way that damages minority viewpoints and calcifies the art of interpretation. Only the quirkiness of considered individual expression can cut through the nonsense of mob – and that is the reason intellectual activity is important. [...] Web 2.0 adherents might respond to these objections by claiming that I have confused individual expression with intellectual achievement. This is where we find our greatest point of disagreement. I am amazed by the power of the collective to enthral people to the point of blindness. Collectivists adore a computer operating system called LINUX, for instance, but it is really only one example of a descendant of a 1970s technology called UNIX. If it weren't produced by a collective, there would be nothing remarkable about it at all. Meanwhile, the truly remarkable designs that couldn't have existed 30 years ago, like the iPhone, all come out of 'closed' shops where individuals create something and polish it before it is released to the public.[1]

I appreciate the fact that Lanier places his accent on the necessity to orient the possibilities of technology towards the world of culture and to creativity, rather than vice versa. Optimists like Clay Shirky justly see in the collaboration made possible by internet a growing potential of culture. They tend, however, to underestimate the need to organize this collaboration. And that means the necessity of placing an external point to the system – the creative person – which no collaboration can ever eliminate.

□ □ □

IV

EDUCATION

For most of us, this is the aim
Never here to be realised;
Who are only undefeated
Because we have gone on trying.

T.S. Eliot, *The Dry Salvages,* V

In this fourth section I would like to look at education. If all the problems I talked about exist, what can we do?

Above all we must learn to *identify* the issues. This means learning to judge with criteria that are not taken from the same technologies we would like to judge.[1] Efficiency, being reachable, speed and frequency of communication: all of these elements must be judged by each of us on the basis of other criteria, for example the depth and the richness of our relationships.

What follows is not a recipe but a description of an attempt at education in the Catholic seminary I teach in. We aim at keeping together the need to learn a strong, joyful and vivid freedom that encourages curiosity and is unafraid of modernity, with the spiritual needs of priestly life. Given the particular character of a seminary, it is obvious that not all of what we do can by copied by other groups. But I think that our attempt is in large measure similar to what parents can do with their children, and teachers can do with their students. In the end, true education aims always at augmenting the freedom of the student, in view of the Good. It has to indicate an ideal and offer the instruments to work towards it.

□ □ □

16

EVERY PLACE IS UNIQUE

More than any other writer Wendell Berry helped me to find a reasonable equilibrium between criticizing and accepting the world in which I live. One of the first texts which I read by Berry was this:

> To confess, these days, that you think some things are more important than machines is almost sure to bring you face to face with somebody who will accuse you of being 'against technology' – against, that is, 'the larger, more efficient business organization' that will emerge inevitably 'to the benefit of the many.' And so I would like to be as plain as possible. What I am against – and without a minute's hesitation or apology – is our slovenly willingness to allow machines and the idea of the machine to prescribe the terms and conditions of the lives of creatures, which we have allowed increasingly for the last two centuries, and are still allowing, at an incalculable cost to other creatures *and to ourselves*. If we state the problem that way, then we can see that the way to correct our error, and so deliver ourselves from our own destructiveness, is to quit using our technological capability as the reference point and standard of our economic life. We will instead have to measure our economy by the health of the ecosystems and human communities where we do our work.[1]

Berry wants to subvert the fatalism of those who have given up on judging. We are not robots in an evolutionary mechanism, proceeding on cosmic roads of progress. We are free beings. It is up to us to decide the criteria of our actions, not some imaginary 'invisible hand'.

Berry defends love for local reality, which is none other than the reality in which each and every one of us lives. We do not have to follow him in going 'back to the land', nonetheless Berry teaches us to learn to love every square inch of our world; the place where we live and work, and the real people who inhabit it are more authentic than the infinite and incorporeal dimensions of the internet, and a whole lot more stimulating.

Berry is an innovative thinker and although his ideas remain at first a little difficult to share, his literary prose has a beguiling power. *Jayber Crow*, his masterpiece, is the novel that most profoundly convinced me. It is set in Port William, a country town of no particular importance, and written from perspective of the barber, whose name gives the title to the book. Slowly but surely we find ourselves drawn into the microscopic world of the town, made up of few people and even fewer goings on, but in which many shades of the life experience are gradually revealed: honour and baseness, love and egoism, humour and suffering. And as we begin to learn of the work of the townsfolk, their relationships, their arguments and their laughter, we find ourselves looking at our own lives with new eyes, with more patience and more compassion.

I could see in Berry's characters some of the people I know in my own town, or in the parishes in Italy where I live and work. I saw them no longer with the haste of one who wants to move on, to do something else, something Important, but with a tenderness of one who sees that life is brief, that every person is a miracle, and that all of creation is an immense gift. As I observed these changes in myself and in the way I treated others, I recognized that it was for the better. Berry had the same self-revelation:

'Through an imaginary place I learned to see my native place, and my neighbourhood as a unique place in the whole world, a work of God.'

Certainly a novel is not enough to change one's life completely, but it did change my value judgment about my small world. Berry encouraged me to see the positive side of regionalism, as expressed in local tastes and customs which even depend on the side of the river upon which certain foods are seasoned, or the specific rocky wall of the mountains where grapes are grown for wine. He made me perceive the immense richness in every specific place. Nothing is the same as anything else, everything and everyone is unique.

Still immersed in the world of Berry, reading his collection of essays entitled *The Way of Ignorance* further enriched my reflections. Here the author insists many times on the limits of man and of creation, and by way of an explanation for the risky title of the collection, he writes:

> Because ignorance is thus a part of our creaturely definition, we need an appropriate way: a way of ignorance, which is the way of neighbourly love, kindness, caution, care, appropriate scale, thrift, good work, right livelihood. Creatures who have armed themselves with the power of limitless destruction should not be following any way laid out by their limited knowledge and their unseemly pride in it. The way of ignorance, therefore, is to be careful, to know the limits and the efficacy of our knowledge. It is to be humble and to work on an appropriate scale.[2]

This apparently obvious idea is in contradiction with what I implicitly thought, that is, that limits are an impediment to my self-realization. When I started to care for the lemon trees in my garden, I experienced how small the space is that a man can care for alone. How heavy a shovel is, how fragile the life of a lemon tree is. I saw limits I could not get away from, and that they were very reasonable, much more reasonable that I was, with my dreams of greatness and efficiency.

In a world which moves along an ever more efficient path, which in its faculties of economy and marketing attempts to homologate desires and human behaviour in order to distribute and sell an ever more homogeneous product, what can we do? With regard to agriculture and ecology, two themes which preoccupied Berry, he wrote:

> I have no large solution to offer. There is, as maybe we all have noticed, a conspicuous shortage of large-scale corrections for problems that have large-scale causes. Our damages to watersheds and ecosystems will have to be corrected one farm, one forest, one acre at a time. The aftermath of a bombing has to be dealt with one corpse, one wound at a time. And so the first temptation to avoid is the call for some sort of revolution.[3]

There is no grand solution, because every situation, every place and every person is unique.

□ □ □

CASE STUDY: THE SEMINARY

At the dawn of the new millennium almost none of our seminarians had a portable laptop computer. There was one email address for everybody – cdfseminaristi@libero.it – and there was a 'mailman' who downloaded and delivered the messages to their recipients (He was a curious guy and sometimes he read the contents of the letters!) There was not even an internet connection in the house, and while the general secretary had a rather slow modem, nobody else really needed one. Cell phones were forbidden, but in reality not too many suffered, because cell phones had only recently entered the pockets of most people.

Ten years on and the situation is radically different. Everyone without exception has a computer in their room. Everyone has a cell phone, everyone has relationships with faraway friends by email, and uses the web. We have had to hire a technician for the internal network that in the meantime we have installed. These changes have brought with them new difficulties. Laptop computers which were once barely enough to write reports for school, now in all cases permit their users to view films and connect to the wireless network which is present in the classrooms of the university, and which the city of Rome will soon make available in our neighbourhood to freely navigate the internet.

For decades in the seminary we have proposed one film a week because we think that cinema is an important artistic language, but that it must not substitute other forms of human relationships, playing music together, conversation, card games, theatre. We have noted, however, that new seminarians entering today are used to watching three or four films a week. With the possibility of seeing films in their rooms they continue to live as before.

The same is true for other tools. If in 2002 we allowed our seminarians to have cell phones in order to adapt to a cultural change which made them useful and almost indispensable, we have noticed the downside of their omnipresence. Long distance relationships, because they are now possible, take up more and more time, to the detriment of local relationships. The same we can say for internet and email. Time and attention which would be better dedicated to other things is spent surfing dozens of news sites or watching inane videos on YouTube. I observed all these changes without reaching a clear judgment about them. They were gradual, and almost invisible because they seemed innocuous, yet they had a profound effect on the life of the community. For that reason, the directors of the seminary and I decided to face these issues directly in a series of lectures, and also take the dramatic steps towards initiating a 'technological fast'.

In the Christian tradition, fasting is an instrument of consciousness. Voluntarily limiting one's consumption of food, a person learns that he or she depends on God. It is enough to spend a few hours without eating to perceive that one is not autonomous. The priorities in life are thus re-ordered, and a person even delights in the taste of a simple piece of bread. One perceives one is humble and weak, dependent on God for everything, even for simple things like water, as well as discovering or re-discovering the intimate link between body and spirit.

Therefore, we put a proposal to all first year seminarians, to live for 365 days without a laptop and without a cell phone, in order to learn the true value of these tools, to concentrate themselves on what is essential. Freedom and consciousness need an education. For this reason, it was necessary to accompany the structural changes with a community reflection, which we did for four months, with one lesson a month and many conversations in between.

Before I started giving these lessons, one of the seminarians, a talkative Roman student with whom I have a frank and open friendship, asked me: 'Isn't this like a castration?' Exactly the misunderstanding to avoid. Education must not be castration: on the contrary, it must make our freedom stronger. Some people have the idea that religious communities live out of pure irrational obedience, but that is not the case. We believe that where freedom is not sustained by reason, asceticism flounders, or is taken to a libertine extreme. While I asked my seminarian friend to trust me, I didn't pretend to force him to obey me blindly, but to have a cordial willingness to see if he was able to verify my assertions in his own life.

When I began the first lesson, the hostility toward me was palpable! So I simply described the difficulties that I experience with technology, while insisting on the values of the spiritual life and freedom. And I explained why we thought this change of course was necessary. In the following weeks, during many meals together, I saw most of the doubts disappear. After the first lesson, my roman friend came back to me to say 'thank you', not so much because he had already agreed with everything but because he saw that I was sincerely involved with the same problems and desirous to live better together with the rest of them. We have to learn our limits in a climate of freedom, with realism and without being disingenuous. I said, 'Fences are not enough to save your soul. I am not primarily interested in avoiding sin but in educating your freedom. You have a personal decision to make: how are you using your time? At the university when you bring your laptop, do you really study better? During the lessons aren't you tempted to connect to your email or to look for something on Google or to chat with a friend? Is all this a help or an impediment for your studies?'

It is too early to judge the long term consequences of our technological fast, but I am comforted that other seminaries, for example the diocesan seminary of Denver in the United States, which has had a relationship with technology for a longer time than us, have come to the same conclusions. I was impressed when I met some of their seminarians by the joyful and mature relationship that they had with their gadgets. But beyond the long term usefulness of this education which depends in a large measure on the choices of each one of us, what has grown between us is a more explicit and critical understanding of what we think is essential in our lives. And this is already a liberation. To paraphrase Wendell Berry, we are learning to evaluate our lives not based on our technological expertise, but on the basis of the health of our human community.

□ □ □

18

FENCES AND OPEN PRAIRIES

I already said that limits, 'fences', are not enough to safeguard the Good. They are, however, almost the only practical tool around to help control and moderate the use of the internet. Usually these filters try to define the amount of time a user can access the web, which websites he visits and the type of content he engages with.

A couple of years ago I taught physics in a high school in America. While I was there, the school purchased a laptop for every student. They also installed a wireless network which was very sophisticated and very fast; it permitted the students to access the internet protected by filters which were continuously being updated. Too bad that American students are generally quicker at cracking filters than the filter companies are in updating their software! With the help of anonymizer.com and other proxy servers updated every few minutes, they were able to go outside the fences and run happily through the prairies of Facebook and YouTube, while yours truly gave his lesson.

In truth, I do not think that my job as a teacher was much different than that of my own teachers twenty years before. If in my day we used a pen as a spitball shooter, today my students could send each other absurd and amusing YouTube films, and the song hits of the moment. For that reason I was not scandalized that my high school students wanted to fool their professor. At the same time, I do not think it is reasonable to hope a filter, however sophisticated it might be, can eliminate a student's distraction. It would be like obliging Bic to make pens with little holes drilled in the side, in such a way that they could not be úsed to shoot spitballs. The students would simply choose to use a different type of pen!

One of the jobs of a teacher is to maintain order. And as in a family, where many mothers and fathers complain about the difficulties they have limiting use of the internet, television and computer games – the responsibility cannot in the end be relegated to censor organs or filters. The parents must be responsible for the education of their children. And while they can be helped by filters, they must not have the illusion that these filters could substitute their loving and authoritative presence.

The fact that all of this is of great importance is clear from the news that the papers carry almost daily. We read about a kid in Genova[1] who needed police intervention to stop his addiction to computer games, or a fifteen year girl who hung herself when her parents took away her cell phone.[2] A father near Milan who had to be hospitalized because of his internet addiction …[3] The internet has a phenomenology similar to social drugs. Alcohol has been regulated but that has not eliminated alcoholism. Maturing our freedom is the most urgent goal of education.

□ □ □

19

TECHNOLOGICAL FAST

'A fast?! But now we have internet, we have to live with it, we cannot go back to the middle ages …'

Certainly we cannot go back to the middle ages, nor do we want to. On the contrary we want to learn freedom. It will probably seem contradictory to speak of fasting – isn't that a prime example of 'putting up fences'? Isn't that eliminating the possibility of mistakes by eliminating freedom? It would be if it were an end in itself. But fasting is not a long term solution. It is just a pedagogical tool.

But, once again, let's take this one step at a time.

Freedom means to live what is essential, not losing oneself in too much detail, not floating on the surface of sensation. The 'technological fast' which I propose to the new seminarians who enter our seminary is designed to favour their prayer life and the growth of human relationships. Most of them have never lived without computers, television or cell phones. They need to experience that not only is it possible, but sometimes it can be more rewarding to live in this way. They need to savour their prayer as an encounter with God, which is infinitely more satisfying than any film, video game, chat conversation, or web surf. They need to immerse themselves in the new relationships with the other seminarians, which can be more difficult if they are too involved in external relationships.

By now it must be obvious that the ideal in which I believe is that proposed by the Catholic Church. But my reasoning here is not sectarian. Even someone who does not believe in God recognizes priorities in their values – certain relationships, activities, and books are more important, others less. It is not essential for my argument that we share the same list of priorities.

All of us need to begin from what is essential in order to live that which is secondary as an enrichment and not as an obstacle in our lives. If to safeguard and properly engage with the goods which we consider most precious (in my case, our human relationships, prayer and contemplation) it is necessary to separate ourselves from other goods, we need to have the necessary freedom to make this separation. A 'fast' can be good practice.

It might seem like an impossible proposal. We are already connected with our iPhones 24 hours, 7 days a week. Many jobs cannot even be done any more without the rapidity of connections, the mobility and infrastructure our technological gadgets offer us. Even writing this I am taking advantage of a laptop to work in the peace of the Tuscan countryside. But like when we fast from food, we continue to eat bread and drink water, I am not talking about taking away altogether something essential. I don't want to be ideologically closed in the refusal of everything that has an 'on switch'. Nor do I mean to judge most of the tools of the modern day world of work as immoral; many jobs require the constant use of technology, and asking one not to use them would be a violence.

Instead, my proposal has to do with ordering the spaces which are left free, and to judge our tools on the basis of their purpose. A 'fast', therefore, could very simply be turning off our cell phones when we are at table with friends and family, to prefer their real presence to the messages, emails or telephone calls that could arrive in the meantime.

A fast can open a space of freedom and judgment, but a fast alone is not enough. On the first level of importance we must place an ideal, and not just the question: 'So can I use the

internet/ my palm pilot/my cell phone and so forth?' The technical question must be secondary, defined by an ideal. We do not
need a case-by-case manual. We need criteria for personal judgment.

The answer to the question: 'So can I use it?' is a series of
further questions: Who do you live for? What is truly important in
your life? Is Facebook a way to live your relationships better? If so,
wonderful. Or does it become an exercise of your vanity, an
impoverishment of quality into quantity? Maybe it would be
better to leave it alone, then. Does your cell phone free you or
enslave you? And so forth for your iPad, your laptop, and
your blog.

To educate is to help 'incarnate' the ideal in concrete reality.
The work of an educator, of a father, of a mother consists of this:
to live an ideal which is convincing for themselves and to then
propose it to their sons, daughters or their students. One needs a
guide to lead by the hand inside the dynamics of existence. At the
same time, that guide must also give the criteria necessary for
personal judgment, and for a serious critique of those very same
criteria. In the end one's children and students will have to decide
for themselves. But if they do not receive an attractive and
plausible ideal to start with they will more easily be lost.

Therefore it seems the only road possible is freedom, oriented
by a great ideal. Men and women must decide for the good
because they are deeply convinced that is better for them to do so.
Only an ideal that is both beautiful and plausible has the requisite
strength. It must be beautiful: it must have an attractive force, it
must be more appealing than the alternatives. And it must be
plausible, otherwise it will only be an illusion, little different
from any drug, and which if it soon does not give way to another
more realistic 'ideal', will end up swallowing up part of our
humanity.[1]

I found a similar concept in an interview with Neil Postman on YouTube (of course!).[2] In summary, he says, faced with any gadget to ask yourself three questions: 1. What does this thing promise, what problems will it solve? 2. Am I interested in its promise? Do I really have these problems? 3. What other problems will it create?

We don't need to demonize or give general absolutions to anything, but we do need to judge. And sometimes, as Frodo came to discover, we might arrive at the conclusion that some rings are better not worn.

V

□ □ □

CONCLUSION

When, one day, through a door slightly ajar
among the trees of a courtyard
we are shown the yellows of lemons;
and the freezing heart thaws,
and in our breast their songs cascade
golden trumpets of sunshine.

Eugenio Montale, *I limoni*

□ □ □

20

THE RING AND THE CROSS

I would like to conclude with a few words on the current position of the Catholic Church about the usage of communication technologies.

There have been many discourses and many conventions, and many books which I don't mean to cover in detail here – the Pope's talks have been more interesting and more concise. In 2009 Benedict XVI gave a beautiful discourse which put in evidence the desire of communion which the new means of communication express:

> Desire for communication and friendship is rooted in our very nature as human beings and cannot be adequately understood as a response to technical innovations. In the light of the biblical message, it should be seen primarily as a reflection of our participation in the communicative and unifying Love of God, who desires to make of all humanity one family.[1]

This desire seems to me the point where we should aim our attention. Rather than on the technical methodology, which in any case rapidly changes and which must constantly be re-learned, we need to look at the deep reasons which push men and women to search for new means of communication. And then we must evaluate the efficacy of these means of creating and strengthening the communion which we were looking for.

Two years later the same Benedict XVI expressed himself with more cautious tones in his discourse for the International Day of Social Communications:

> Who is my 'neighbour' in this new world? Does the danger exist that we may be less present to those whom we encounter in our everyday life? Is there is a risk of being more distracted because our attention is fragmented and absorbed in a world 'other' than the one in which we live? Do we have time to reflect critically on our choices and to foster human relationships which are truly deep and lasting? It is important always to remember that virtual contact cannot and must not take the place of direct human contact with people at every level of our lives.[2]

In reality he was not saying anything other than what the *Verbum Domini* says:

> Among the new forms of mass communication, nowadays we need to recognize the increased role of the *internet*, which represents a new forum for making the Gospel heard. Yet we also need to be aware that the virtual world will never be able to replace the real world, and that evangelization will be able to make use of the *virtual world* offered by the new media in order to create meaningful relationships only if it is able to offer the *personal contact* which remains indispensable.[3]

It seems to me, beyond the need for a solid foundation in anthropology and a serious critical judgment regarding the conclusions we have come to, there is also another difficulty in the emphasis that certain parts of the Church have given to 'social communications'. Emphasizing mass communication, or virtual communication, sometimes we run the risk of underestimating the greatest novelty the Church has to offer, which is the mystery of the Incarnation. God become man, the ideal made concrete: now that really is new! That really is communion! It seems to me highly meaningful that God chose a moment in history to incarnate himself, in which mass communication did not exist. And what is more, he did not write anything. He decided to entrust the entire future of His church to the person-to-person witness of his disciples. He was willing to run the risk of mediation, that his message be communicated by other people's words. It is true this witness very soon found written form, but let us remember that *sola scriptura* is not enough. The correct interpretation of scripture can only happen within living tradition.

The history of the Church is full of fine examples of people like St Paul, who tried to communicate ideas about their faith with the new forms of communication of the time. I am also thinking of the scribes who copied pages and pages of manuscript, as well as more recent television evangelizers including the American Fulton Sheen, or the incredible energy of the Polish priest Maximilian Kolbe, who founded radio stations and news-papers which printed millions of copies with huge printing presses – he even founded cities before his death as a martyr in Auschwitz. Finally let us remember the incredible influence of John Paul II or Mother Theresa: they had a luminous and convincing presence even on the television screen. Yet I cannot but add: these people's actions have born true fruit according to the measure in which they favoured interpersonal relationships in the flesh, in small, local communities.

Would confession by telephone, fax, email or chat be the same thing, with respect to the encounter with divine mercy through the priest present? Wouldn't it be much more abstract and cold (besides being invalid)? Can you ask your girlfriend to marry you over Skype? It seems to me that virtual communication can be a support to relationships, but it cannot make them grow and mature with the speed, depth and honesty that physical communication can guarantee.

Another Church document produced by the Pontifical Council for Social Communications in 2002 says: 'virtual reality cannot substitute the real presence of Christ in the Eucharist, the sacramental reality of the other sacraments and the liturgical celebrations participated in a human community in flesh and blood. On the internet there are no sacraments.' In other words, it seems like the fundamental problem for Catholics is not so much conquering the spaces of the web for Christ, but rather to live with Christ and the Church in the sacraments. Those who do so will 'Christify' every place in which they live, including the internet.[4]

I mentioned the theme of power already, when I spoke about *The Lord of the Rings*. It is an example which can help us, because the ring of power offers us an easily understood symbol of a problem which can be extremely complicated. In Tolkien's novel the ring could theoretically be a useful tool for the cause of Good, but there's a twist: the ring and its power fatally become the centre of the affections of the person who uses it. You cannot use the ring and remain untouched. Moreover, it is a dilemma one cannot simply resolve by renouncing every relationship with power. We cannot avoid the risk of power by eliminating it. But how can we live with it?

The example of salvation which was brought through Christ helps us to understand that we must not start from Faustian conquests of technology, asking ourselves how the Church can use these conquests for its mission. We must begin with the divine power of the Word who worked our salvation through the cross, revealing himself in the vulnerability of love.[5]

All this leaves us with a significant question: why did God, who is omnipotent, let himself be nailed so cruelly to the cross? Why didn't he unleash his legions of angels, and instead prefer igno-miny and irrelevance to the hegemony of force?

□ □ □

21

POWER IS LOVE

In 1966 genius-pessimist Martin Heidegger gave an interview to *Der Spiegel*.[1] He spoke in particular of technology and its meaning for human life.

> There is an idea that technology is in its essence something human beings have under their control. In my opinion, that is not possible. Technology is in its essence something that human beings cannot master of their own accord.

Toward the end of the interview some very surprising ideas emerged, almost like an oracle:

> Only a god can still save us. I think the only possibility of salvation left to us is to prepare readiness, through thinking and poetry, for the appearance of the god or for the absence of the god during the decline.

Heidegger speaks as an atheist and this can explain how his words have a depressing abyssal flavour – decline being apparently inevitable, without any God able to appear on the scene and save us. The best thing we can do is live our lives as stoics.

Heidegger had however identified with precision the condition for a rebirth:

> From our human experience and history, at least as far as I
> am informed, I know that everything essential and great has
> only emerged when human beings had a home and were
> rooted in a tradition.

But he did not believe in it any more. How can we recover a home
and a tradition?

In reality 'the God' has already come, and he has already taught
us the road for rebirth. The true worth of this road is made clear in
a particularly elegant manner by Benedict of Norcia, who lived at
a time at least as bewildering as our own. Furthermore, he had to
deal with the collapse of an august civilization, the barbarian
invasions and widespread egoism among governing classes. And
Benedict with his singular intuition of the '*unicum necessarium*' and
his balanced roman spirit laid the foundations of Europe. He
profoundly lived the 'home' and the 'tradition' of which
Heidegger speaks. And something essentially great and grandiose
emerged from his experience. His faith in human and social
change, which came about through involving his own work in the
work of God, and through the orientation of his heart and mind in
prayer, brought greater fruits than he could have possibly hoped.
He did not intend to re-found the European continent by leaving
his bourgeois roman existence, but in the end that is what he did.

'The God' has already come. And precisely the God Incarnate,
who carried in himself the suffering, death and difficulty of using
power in his sacrifice. Power can only be dominated by love,
which is in essence the sacrifice of one's self for another. Only a
God can save us because only a God can indicate the path in which
power does not consume all that is good and beautiful. He has
taught us that power is love, not violence.

All of this indicates that we need to imitate the same behaviour
in our relationship with the power of technology. Only if we learn
to receive reality as a gift can we overcome the mere 'use' of it

which impoverishes and empties the world. Technology cannot give order to life, it is life that must order technology. The dominion of which Genesis speaks is not arbitrary but is in accord with being. Being is gift, not robbery. Being is love.

In summary I affirm the world is already beautiful the way it is. We do not need to create new worlds, it is more to live fully in this one. The shades of meaning in human relationships, even the more simple shades, are incommensurably richer than any virtual mediation of those relationships. Virtuality can serve the human community, but it cannot substitute it.

Let us consider as well the overabundance of nature: the scent of lemons, the flavours of our food, the perfume of flowers, the green hues of our trees, the majestic banks of clouds, the sparkling light on the water, the solemn silence of the mountains, the various and fascinating world of animals … It does not necessarily follow that mankind's constructions be opposed to nature. One glance at the English or Tuscan countryside is enough to convince us of the opposite truth. We need, however, to order these constructions according to nature, respecting the order already there rather than imposing our iron will on the world. The physicist Richard Feynman said: 'in order for a technology to be successful it is important that reality have precedence on public relations, because you cannot fool nature'. I too believe reality does not betray us.

So all in all, I hope I have been clear. I do not want to fire off any fatwas or anathemas against cell phones or the internet. I do not oppose the use of technology, I just want to order it to the deep rhythms of our existence. What I am against is the unconditional surrender to fatalism and the ingenuous hope of social evolutionism, and the pusillanimity of those who content themselves with complaining about the things that are not going well, without proposing a better road. I firmly believe that a better road exists, and that God taught it to us in Jesus Christ. He does not have to come back again to teach us one more time. We just have to follow the road that he has already indicated, and which many times has brought unexpected fruits in seemingly desperate times. It is up to us to build relationships and homes, to root ourselves in a tradition, and to work.

NOTES

1 Beginnings

1 http://blog.nielsen.com/nielsenwire/online_mobile/u-s-teen-mobile-report-calling-yesterday-texting-today-using-apps-tomorrow/

3 The Problem

1 One of the few writers who combines a profound critique of modernity with an ultimately positive view of things is Romano Guardini. One beautiful passage is in the closing pages of *The End of the Modern World*, where he writes: 'The free union of the human person with the Absolute through unconditional freedom will enable the faithful to stand firm – God-centered – even though placeless and unprotected. It will enable man to enter into an immediate relationship with God which will cut through all force and danger. It will permit him to remain a vital person within the mounting loneliness of the future, a loneliness experienced in the very midst of the masses and all their organizations. […] Loneliness in faith will be terrible. Love will disappear from the face of the public world, but the more precious will be that love which flows from one lonely person to another, involving a courage of the heart born from the immediacy of the love of God as it was made known in Christ. Perhaps man will come to experience this love anew, to taste the sovereignty of its origin, to know its independence of the world, to sense the mystery of its final why? Perhaps love will achieve an intimacy and harmony never known to this day.' Romano Guardini, *The End of the Modern World* (Wilmington DE, ISI Books, 2001), pp. 108–9.

2 In *Walden*, Thoreau wrote: 'We are in great haste to construct a magnetic telegraph from Maine to Texas; but Maine and Texas, it may be, have nothing important to communicate … We are eager to tunnel under the Atlantic and bring the old world some weeks nearer to the new; but perchance the first news that will leak through into the broad flapping American ear will be that Princess Adelaide has the whooping cough.' Cited in N. Postman, *Amusing Ourselves to Death* (New York, Penguin, 2005), p. 65.

3   J.R.R. Tolkien, *The Lord of the Rings. Part One. The Fellowship of the Ring* (New York, Ballantine Books, 1965), p. 410.

4   David L. Schindler, *Ordering Love* (Grand Rapids MI, Eerdmans, 2011).

4   *The Technology of the Book*

1   Nicholas Carr, *The Shallows* (New York, W. W. Norton, 2010), pp. 5–6.

2   Maryanne Wolf, *Proust and the Squid* (London and New York, Harper Perennial 2007), p. 229. She also speaks of 'delay neurons': 'In our brain there are "delay neurons" whose sole function is to slow neuronal transmission by other neurons for mere milliseconds. These are the inestimable milliseconds that allow sequence and order in our apprehension of reality, and that enable us to plan and synchronize soccer moves and symphonic movements.' (pp. 213–14).

3   Carr, *The Shallows*, p. 9.

4   Carr, *The Shallows*, p. 134–5. The original research is here: http://www.useit.com/alertbox/reading_pattern.html

5   See http://lindastone.net/

5   *Reading and Writing*

1   Neurogenesis is a fascinating topic, but is still little understood. For the purposes of this affirmation, I am referring to the data available in a common textbook, M. F. Bear, B. W. Connors and M. Paradiso, *Neuroscience: Exploring the Brain*, 3rd edn (Baltimore MD, Lippincott Williams and Wilkins, 2007), p. 693.

2   These exciting discoveries have been recounted in passionate detail by Norman Doidge in his *The Brain that Changes Itself* (New York, Penguin, 2007). The writer, a psychiatrist and researcher at Columbia University in New York, reconstructs the history of the fundamental discoveries in neuroscience by presenting various 'case studies' of his personal knowledge. Five years earlier, Jeffrey Schwartz and Sharon Begley told the same story in more technical language in *The Mind and the Brain* (London and New York, HarperCollins, 2002).

3   I refer to Eric Kandel's famous experiment using *Aplysia,* which earned him the Nobel Prize in 2000. He electrically stimulated a sea-slug repeatedly, and noted that its reaction diminished with the experience. The animal's nervous system is so simple that Kandel was able to discover the changes on the level of individual neurons and synapses which corresponded to the change in behaviour.

4   Described in Schwartz and Begley, *The Mind and the Brain*, p. 217.

5   Carr, *The Shallows*, p. 48.

6   http://lindastone.net/2010/10/20/the-look-feel-of-conscious-computing/

7   Stanislas Dehaene, *Reading in the Brain* (New York, Penguin, 2009), p. 10.

6   Tools are not Neutral

1   Neil Postman, *Amusing Ourselves to Death* (New York, Penguin, 1985), p. 7.
2   Marshall McLuhan, *Understanding Media* (Berkeley CA, Gingko Press, 2003), p. 23

7   Evolution of the Species

1   Kevin Kelly, *What Technology Wants*, (New York, Viking, 2010).
2   Kelly, p. 349.
3   Kelly, p. 359.

10   Irreproducibility

1   Walter Benjamin, 'L'opera d'arte nell'epoca della sua riproducibilità tecnica' (*Einaudi*, 1966), pp. 22–3.
2   Adam Briggle, 'Dear Facebook' in D. E. Wittkower (ed.) *Facebook and Philosophy* (Chicago, Carus Publishing, 2010), p. 168.

13   Pornified

1   http://www.internet-filter-review.toptenreviews.com/internet-pornography-statistics.html
2   Norman Doidge, *The Brain that Changes Itself* (New York, Penguin, 2007), pp. 106–9.
3   Federico Tonioni, interview with the author.

15   Creativity and Collectivization

1   See http://www.amazon.com/You-Are-Not-Gadget-Manifesto/dp/0307269647

IV   Education

1   George Grant, an excellent Canadian philosopher, said something similar in his very early articles commenting on the meaning of the computer revolution. In 1987 he wrote: 'When we represent technology to ourselves through its own common sense we think of ourselves as picking and choosing in a supermarket, rather than within the analogy of the package deal. We have bought a package deal

of far more fundamental novelness than simply a set of instruments under our control. It is a destiny which enfolds us in its own conceptions of instrumentality, neutrality, and purposiveness. It is in this sense that it has been truthfully said: technology is the ontology of the age. Western peoples (and perhaps soon all peoples) take themselves as subjects confronting otherness as objects – objects lying as raw material at the disposal of knowing and making subjects. Unless we comprehend the package deal we obscure from ourselves the central difficulty in our present destiny: we apprehend our destiny by forms of thought which are themselves the very core of that destiny.' George Parkin Grant, 'Thinking about Technology,' in *Technology and Justice* (Notre Dame IN, University of Notre Dame Press, 1987).

16 Every Place is Unique

1   Wendell Berry, *Life is a Miracle* (Berkeley CA, Counterpoint, 2001), p. 54.
2   Wendell Berry, *The Way of Ignorance* (Berkeley CA, Counterpoint, 2005), p. ix.
3   Berry, *Life is a Miracle,* pp. 62–3.

18 Fences and Open Prairies

1   http://www.corriere.it/cronache/10_giugno_13/genova-playstation_147d098a-76bf-11df-9f61–00144f02aabe.shtml
2   http://www.corriere.it/cronache/09_maggio_12/cellulare_punizione_impiccato_c4a2a252–3ec6–11de-914a-00144f02aabc.shtml
3   http://www.aipsimed.org/articolo/schiavo-di-internet-sfascia-la-famiglia

19 Technological Fast

1   On this theme, the sometimes hilariously politically incorrect British philosopher, Roger Scruton wrote: 'There are powers which cannot be used to further our goals, but which on the contrary provide our goals and limit them: such are the powers contained in a genuine culture – the redemptive powers of love and judgement. To be subject to these powers is not to be enslaved, but on the contrary to realise a part of human freedom. It is to rise above the realm of means, into the kingdom of ends – into the ideal world which is made actual by our aspiration.' Roger Scruton, *An Intelligent Person's Guide to Modern Culture* (South Bend IN, St Augustine's Press, 2000), p. 131–2.
2   http://www.youtube.com/watch?v=49rcVQ1vFAY

20   The Ring and the Cross

1   http://www.vatican.va/holy_father/benedict_xvi/messages/
     communications/documents/hf_ben-xvi_mes_20090124_43rd-world-
     communications-day_en.html

2   http://www.svdcuria.org/public/communic/docs/1101cday.htm

3   http://www.zenit.org/article-30942?l=english

4   Antonio Spadaro, director of *La Civiltà Cattolica* and widely read blogger, gave an
     interview to Andrea Monda which was published in *Il Foglio*, 5 February 2011. He
     said: 'This is the real challenge: to learn to be wired in a fluid, natural, ethical and
     even spiritual way; live the net as an environment for life.' He then raises the
     interesting problem of the sacraments: it is clear that we can never eliminate the
     physical reality of bread and wine in the Mass, but we should still reflect upon the
     fact that digital technology has created a 'new space of experience, which the
     Christian liturgy should take into account'. It seems to me that the form of the
     sacraments is surprisingly universal precisely because they do not require special
     materials or experiences, but are connected to experiences which every person
     can have: bread, water, oil, wine … The Net is not a fundamental experience. It is
     an important superstructure, but it cannot be equated with physical reality, the
     only 'space of experience' in which the *whole* human person, body and soul, lives
     and has relationships.

5   H. U. von Balthasar is enlightening on this point: 'Why should the children of the
     shadows eternally be wiser than the children of the light? We must beat them in
     their own home ground, consecrate more deeply to God the worldly forces; not
     through renunciation, but through their use make them bear fruit for the reign of
     God, contribute to the fulfillment of His will not only in heaven but also on earth.
     This program of Christian progressivism is surprisingly close to its mortal
     adversary, Christian integralism. While the second tends to occupy the places of
     earthly power, in order to announce from that pulpit the teachings of the
     Beatitudes and the Cross, the first makes the positions of the Beatitudes and the
     cross internal agents of the progress of earthly power. At the end, both positions
     resolve the problem of the relationship of power between God and the world,
     between grace and nature, reducing all to a monistic, easily understood form,
     which is accessible to the initiative of men. […] Today we have become capable of
     seeing the superficial and arbitrary character of this solution, but we have become
     insensible to its modern variant, which would like to interpret and exploit in an
     immediately christological fashion the tools of technical power and the so-called
     "reflection of the noosphere" which technique has introduced.' *Il tutto nel fram-
     mento* (Milan, Jaca Book, 1970), p. 174.

21   Power is Love

1   'Nur noch ein Gott kann uns retten,' *Der Spiegel*, 31 May 1976, pp. 193–219.
     The interview with Rudolf Augstein and Georg Wolff took place on 23 September
     1966.